Guts and Go Overtime
More Great Saskatchewan Hockey Stories

Praise for

Guts and Go:
Great Saskatchewan Hockey Stories

"A great read for the hockey-starved fan. This book scores with profiles of many of the most famous Saskatchewan-born NHL players and gets a big assist with stories of lesser-known players and teams."

—Jason Hammond, "Sask Books Go Public," CJTR Radio

MORE GREAT SASKATCHEWAN
Guts and Go
Overtime
HOCKEY STORIES

Guts and Go Overtime

More Great Saskatchewan Hockey Stories

Calvin Daniels

Victoria · Calgary · Vancouver

Heritage House Publishing Company Ltd.
#108 – 17665 66A Avenue
Surrey, BC V3S 2A7
www.heritagehouse.ca

Library and Archives Canada Cataloguing in Publication
Daniels, Calvin, 1960-
Guts and go overtime : more great Saskatchewan hockey stories / Calvin Daniels.
ISBN 1-894974-02-6
1. Hockey--Saskatchewan. 2. Hockey players--Saskatchewan. I. Title.
GV848.5.A1D353 2005 796.962'097124 C2005-904886-7

Edited by Linda Berry and Corina Skavberg
Book design by One Below
Cover design by One Below
Cover photo by (front) Brian Opyd/iStockphoto; (back) Matthew Dula/iStockphoto

Printed in Canada on 100% post-consumer recycled paper.

Heritage House acknowledges the financial support for its publishing program from the Government of Canada through the Book Publishing Industry Development Program (BPIDP), Canada Council for the Arts, and the British Columbia Arts Council.

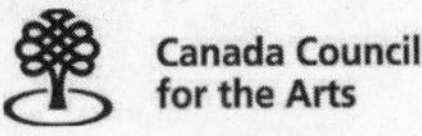

Contents

continued...

Foreword

Sitting down to write a foreword for this book was an experience I never really dared to expect.

It was one thing to write *Guts and Go: Great Saskatchewan Hockey Stories* in early 2004. That was a thrill, which came my way when Heritage House Publishing contacted me just before Christmas in 2003. They had an idea which was so simple, yet compelling for a hockey fan in Saskatchewan. They wanted a history of the game, and more importantly, a history of the people from this province who have contributed to the game.

It was an offer, as they say, too good to refuse.

It was a big project that came together in what seemed almost too short a time as I juggled interviews and writing for the book with my regular career as a journalist.

As much as it was a thrill interviewing the likes of Dave Schultz and Clark Gillies, the bigger thrill was holding the finished book in my hand when it arrived in the mail one day.

It was my second book. *Skating the Edge*, a work of short fiction, was published in 2001, but *Guts and Go* was still special. There is more effort in a sense to a work of non-fiction. The words don't simply flow from your creative thoughts. There is the planning, interviewing and research that precedes the writing process, which relies on the accuracy of getting others' words onto the page.

I'd be amiss here if I didn't thank all those who took the time to allow me to interview them for this work. Without them there would be no book.

My wife Dixie also gets a big thank-you here for all her help in setting up interviews, reading over my work, and always being supportive, even on days I was tired and cranky writing this book.

With the book in my hands, the fun started. There were book signings, and radio, television and newspaper interviews to promote the book. It was an enjoyable experience being on the opposite end of an interview after carrying out hundreds of them myself in some 17 years as a journalist.

Certainly, as you go down the promotions road you hope the book is well-received. I know many friends were quick to pick up the book, but rare is it that a friend picks apart a story, so their view is always a tad flattering.

I know over the days I autographed a lot of books, which in and of itself is a thrill. It's kind of neat that someone would value my scrawled name across a page in a book, even if it is a book I wrote.

With all that being said, as an author, you aren't really aware if the book is selling as expected by the publisher, or whether it is short of their goals. I was aware that sales are the ultimate measure of success.

There was talk as I wrote the first book that a follow-up might be possible. Several weeks into starting to write the first book I recognized there were enough obvious stories to tell about Saskatchewan hockey to fill books two, three and quite likely, four.

Yet I'm not sure how real I thought the dream of doing a follow-up book was. That, I knew, was up to the public. If they bought enough books, I might be back at the computer.

That you are reading this foreword to *Guts and Go Overtime: More Great Saskatchewan Hockey Stories* tells you that book one sold ok. There is a humbling thrill in knowing readers supported the idea and my writing to such a level the publisher felt a follow-up was a good idea.

This book follows the same format as the first. Each chapter is a vignette of someone involved with the beloved game of hockey in Saskatchewan. I hope you find the stories of people such as Jim Neilson, Orland Kurtenbach, Gerry James, Kelly Buchberger, Dick Irvin and all the rest as interesting in reading them as I did in writing them.

I think the amazing thing I have found in the writing of this book, and its predecessor, is that each person who plays hockey, or is connected to it in any way, has a deep devotion to the game. I hope that devotion, that love of hockey permeates this book.

In the end, that love of the game is what connects us, the fans, to those who play the game. We share a passion for the game that brings us together. I just hope this book in some small way contributes to that connection.

Betting on the Broad Street Bullies

Ed Van Impe was a rugged rearguard who stood out on a team noted for its rough and ready style. For nearly nine seasons the Saskatoon-born defenceman was a member of the Philadelphia Flyers during their National Hockey League heyday as the "Broad Street Bullies."

Van Impe said playing the Flyer style was simply his style too. "I handed out a few bumps, and I can tell you I got just as many back." In one game, a puck to the face cost Van Impe six teeth, 35 stitches in his lip, and seven stitches in his tongue, yet after being stitched up, he returned to the game in the third period.

In total he would play 700 regular season NHL games, amassing more than 1,000 penalty minutes, while being named an all-star three times. However, Van Impe's start in hockey was more humble than his NHL days, like that of most young boys in Saskatchewan growing up through the 1940s and '50s. "I don't think I was different from anybody else. I just grew up with it. I started out at a very early age with a rink right in the backyard," he said. In many ways it was a purely cultural thing. "In Canada there's a great deal of interest in hockey."

In Van Impe's case there was also a family connection. "My dad [Frank] played hockey at the senior level, so hockey was something we could enjoy together," he said, adding he never saw his father actually play. "That was before I was old enough to remember. I saw a couple of pictures of him in his hockey uniform, but that was it."

Van Impe's father was a strong influence in his earliest days on ice. "He was very supportive. He was one of those dads that drove whenever they were needed, and he attended most of the practices and games."

From the backyard rink, Van Impe moved to organized hockey, starting at the Pee Wee level in a Saskatoon league sponsored by the Kinsmen Club. "I loved it. My cousins were probably the better players on the team then. I think I probably made it by reputation, my cousins' reputation. I wasn't very good at a young age. I definitely was in the lower half of the team."

While he was not highly skilled as a youth, Van Impe also recalled playing in games pitting players from different public schools against each other. "I remember it was a huge crowd, they were all students like myself, and it was absolutely thrilling."

Van Impe would play minor hockey in his home town, going all the way to Junior in Saskatoon with the Quakers. In fact, he would not leave home until he signed his first professional contract.

In turning pro, Van Impe had no choice of where to go. In those days the NHL team that sponsored the junior team you were on simply owned all the players too. "I grew up signing nothing, but belonging to the Chicago Black Hawks," he said. He kept an eye on the Hawks once he realized he was theirs. "When I realized that I belonged to them, I had a special interest in how they were doing, and some of the players.

"It was a strange environment at that time with only six teams [in the NHL]; somebody almost had to retire for you to be given an opportunity."

So in his first pro season, the Hawks sent Van Impe to Calgary in the Western Hockey League, then to the American Hockey League's Buffalo Bisons for five seasons before breaking him in with the Hawks for the 1965–66 season. "When I was given my opportunity I think there were only seven rookies in the entire league," he said. "Most of us had to spend a few years in the minors before getting a chance."

Van Impe would have a solid season, finishing second in voting for the Calder Trophy as NHL rookie of the year, but it was a distant second to another defenceman—Bobby Orr of the Boston Bruins. Van Impe said Orr was simply in a different class. "Not only did he change hockey for defencemen, he changed hockey totally...He made the rest of us feel pretty darn inadequate."

While finishing second to Orr, Van Impe expected he'd be a Hawk for a while, especially since the team had made the playoffs during his rookie year. The expansion draft was just ahead, when the league would double to 12 teams, but Van Impe said management had assured him he would be protected. But things change. "When I was drafted by Philadelphia with their first pick, I was really disappointed. When I had left Chicago they had told me I'd be one of the defenceman they would protect...I was really disappointed to be starting over with an expansion team," he said.

Time changes the view on many things, and Van Impe now recognizes the move to the Flyers "as the best thing that ever happened to me." Van Impe said the Flyers' organization had a good understanding of the game from the outset. "They built the team on goaltending and defence," he said. Netminders Bernie Parent and Doug Favell, and Van Impe and fellow rearguard Joe Watson were key expansion draft selections.

The rewards of their selections came quickly. The Flyers won the expansion division in their first year, a season that had its hardships, including the roof being blown off the Spectrum in Philadelphia. The Flyers had to play most of their home games in Quebec City.

Then in the playoffs a Flyer flaw became clearly evident. "We just weren't tough enough," said Van Impe. The team lost to St. Louis in the playoffs. "It was fairly obvious we had a lot of skilled players for an expansion team, but they were smaller. Against a big, tough team like St. Louis a lot of our guys were intimidated."

The Philadelphia management took the shortcoming to heart, and went looking to change the team's make-up. "The Flyers were aware of the need for some young, tougher players, and were drafting them. It just took a little while for them to get here, but once they did get here they changed the image of the team dramatically."

The "Broad Street Bullies" were born with the arrival of players such as Saskatchewan-born Dave "the Hammer" Schultz and Don "Big Bird" Saleski, along with Andre "Moose" Dupont and Bob "Battleship" Kelly. "We had three or four guys that teams had to watch—if they tried to take advantage of anyone on our team, they were going to pay the price," said Van Impe, adding that it was a nice change from his perspective. "After playing on a team that wasn't respected, it was a real pleasant change to be part of a team that was respected."

The tough, physical play became an edge for the Flyers, according to Van Impe, who was assigned the Captain's "C" in his second season with the Flyers. Other teams were already in trouble coming into Philadelphia because they felt intimidated. In fact, when Van Impe was traded to Pittsburgh for his final 22 NHL games, he learned that first-hand. "In the dressing room in Philadelphia they were sitting with their heads hanging. We were beat before we got on the ice." He added the trade to the Penguins stung when it came. "The philosophy in Philadelphia was when they figured you'd pretty much had it, and had no upside, they traded you. But I was absolutely stunned when it happened."

Still, when he was with the Flyers, Van Impe was part of a team with a style that the NHL and its president Clarence Campbell did not condone, said Van Impe, yet fans appeared to like the style and that ultimately is what should matter. "Meanwhile everywhere we went we sold out the building. They came out to see the 'Broad Street Bullies.' That was a plain simple fact."

As much as the Flyers were known for a core group of guys who rolled up penalty minutes and intimidated opposition players, the team's gritty style might have been most exemplified by one of the team's best players, future Hall of Famer Bobby Clarke. "He was just a tremendous all-around player," said Van Impe. "... I look at Bobby Clarke as a unique person. He provided leadership by exemplifying hard work...He could not stand to lose. That is the way the Flyers would be known...He had a lot more skills than people give him credit for."

Two other individuals set the Flyers apart during their reign as the NHL tough guys, said Van Impe. One was coach Fred Shero. "The coaching that we had at that time was absolutely outstanding. Fred Shero, he knew what he had and developed a system to work with it," said Van Impe. "...Everybody loved and respected him." The second ace was netminder Bernie Parent, destined for the Hall of Fame, and in Van Impe's mind the best player on the team. "In his era, before his eye injury, he was far and away the best in the league," he said.

The whole thing came together for Van Impe and the Flyers in 1974 when they faced Boston for the Stanley Cup. The Bruins were highly favoured, especially with Hall of Famers Bobby Orr,

Phil Esposito and John Bucyk in the fold. However, people forget the Flyers also had three future Hall of Famers in Parent, Clarke and Bill Barber. Van Impe himself was named to the Flyers' team Hall of Fame in 1993. In the end the rugged Flyers would take the series in six games, with Parent a major factor, including a 1–0 shut out in the deciding sixth game.

"That first Stanley Cup was really unbelievable," said Van Impe. "The first Cup some would say as unexpected...Nobody gave us a chance against Boston. But Fred Shero and the players, we believed we could beat them...

"And it wasn't a fluke. The next year we came back and beat Buffalo, and our style of hockey was not supposed to win."

Of course the "Broad Street Bullies'" style also made international hockey news in 1976, when the Soviet Union team visited the Spectrum. Van Impe would hit Valeri Kharlamov with a huge elbow, and for a time the Russians refused to return to the ice to finish the game. Still, the Russians hadn't lost to an NHL team on their tour until they came up against the physical Flyers, who won 4–1. "I got the feeling they were afraid of us before we started and we didn't disappoint."

"It was probably the most electrifying one game I ever played in," said Van Impe. "...We were absolutely ready to play them."

As for the famous elbow, Van Impe chuckles. "We did win, and it's better to be known for something than for nothing."

The Scout's Eye

Over the years Barry Trapp has developed an eye for hockey talent which has helped him carve out a career which has lasted long after his playing days were over.

"I played all my minor hockey in Balcarres until Midget," he said. "We had a three-team Midget league right in Balcarres. That's pretty amazing considering today small towns have a hard time getting one team together."

In Trapp's era kids had fewer options, so they stayed focused on hockey more. "We didn't have the computers. We didn't have snowmobiles. In the wintertime you either curled, or you played hockey. There were no other distractions. Even television wasn't that big back then with only two channels. You played hockey all day long."

As a Midget, Trapp got lots of ice time, playing not only in Balcarres, but down the road in the provincial capital. "I played Midget in Regina every Saturday. I'd catch a ride with one of dad's trucks and go into Regina every Saturday," he said. His father's business was a trucking firm and as he got older, "that's what I would do all summer. I couldn't wait to come home and drive the big rigs."

By the time Trapp was 15 he was playing senior hockey with the hometown Balcarres Broncs. "It was quite different. The first game of the season would be Boxing Day because we had natural ice," he said. While the senior season was a short one, it was still long enough for Trapp to be noticed by the Melville Millionaires, opening the doors for him to play junior. John Ferguson Sr., then with the Millionaires as their Captain, saw Trapp play and suggested the young rearguard become a Millionaire. Trapp would take up the junior offer, but he would also return to senior hockey in Balcarres after his professional days we're over. His career as a Bronc was only recognized by the team a few years ago when Balcarres retired his #5 sweater. "It was an honour. It was very gratifying to have that done in my hometown."

As a junior in Melville, Trapp said two stories come to mind, and neither of them related to the game of hockey on the ice. Instead, the trials of junior travel conjured the memories. "One year Melville had just bought their first team bus," he said. "We were getting ready to go to Flin Flon and they had this ceremony. The Mayor was there...Father Novak blessed the bus. He walked through the bus and blessed the players, and coaches and the driver.

"We get 10 miles out of town and the bus [breaks down]. We head back into Melville, climb in cars, and head to Flin Flon."

The bus was at the heart of Trapp's second story too. "We were heading to Estevan on Highway #47 by Grenfell," he said remembering the big hill at the valley there. "...We didn't have enough power to get around that last bend, so all the players had to get out and push it the final bit."

Trapp said he enjoyed his time in Melville, a career that

ended with him being named team Captain in his final season as a 20-year-old. "It made me feel so good this season when my grandson Bear [Trapp] was named the Millionaires' Captain as a 20-year-old." The Millionaires faithfully remembered Trapp too, and had a Barry Trapp Night in 1962, even presenting him with a set of golf clubs.

From Melville, the pros beckoned. The Millionaires were at the time supported by the Toronto Maple Leafs, and Trapp was assigned to their farm team in Rochester of the American Hockey League for the 1962-63 season. Trapp would spend five years in the minors with stops in Denver, Victoria and Tulsa, before hanging up his pro dreams. "I was drafted in 1967 by Los Angeles, but I decided it was time to come home."

It was really a decision made on dollars and cents. Trapp said in 1967, the base salary in the NHL was only $12,500, so he saw better opportunities back with the family trucking business. At the same time, Trapp sat in on the first player meeting with Allan Eagleson. Trapp was with LA at the time and said future Hall of Fame netminder Terry Sawchuk came in the room and told players they were meeting with a lawyer, and the meeting focused on players holding out for the minimum of $12,500.

With wages so low in the NHL, Trapp joked there was at least an upside to missing the playoffs or being eliminated early. "If you got beat out early you got home to get the best jobs," he said with a laugh.

Although Trapp would not make the NHL, he did get to play with a number of players who became familiar names in the game, including Pat Quinn, Al Arbour, Gerry Cheevers and Don Cherry. "Al Arbour was my roommate and defensive partner," said Trapp.

As for the flamboyant Cherry, it was Arbour and teammates who gave him the nickname "Sour Grapes." "He [Cherry] was such a miserable b*****d. He was always complaining about something... But he's a tremendous supporter of the Canadian game."

Back home in Balcarres, Trapp played senior hockey again, and concentrated on the trucking business. When he moved to Regina in 1979, fate seemed to take over, and pushed him into the vein of hockey for which he would become best known. "There was an ad in the Regina paper for someone to help coach Midget A hockey a couple of nights a week," he said.

Bob Strumm was helping screen the coaching candidates. He asked to meet with Trapp, and suddenly instead of helping out a couple of nights a week, he was the coach of the Midget AAA Regina Pat Capitals. From there Trapp moved through the local coaching ranks, spending time with the AAA Midget Pat Canadians, the Western Hockey League Regina Pats, and the Moose Jaw Warriors.

Having coached only a limited amount before the AAA Midget opportunity, Trapp said he adapted quickly. "I think AAA Midget is probably the easiest level to coach. They're all gung ho, and willing to learn," he said.

Asked which team stuck out most for Trapp as a coach, he said he remembers them all fondly. "I thought all the teams I had stood out." Still, the WHL Pats took Trapp closest to the top of the pile. "When we lost to Kamloops in the Western final, with only 12 seconds left... We were that close to the Memorial Cup." The Pats led in the dying seconds of Game 6, but Kamloops tied the game and won in overtime, then took Game 7 the next night 3–2. With players like Lyndon Byers and Dale Derkatch on the roster, the loss was a tough one.

In Moose Jaw the talent level was also impressive, with the likes of Lyle Odelein, Kelly Buchberger, Mike Keane and Theoren Fleury, but "it came right down to the wire to just make the playoffs." The Warriors might not have succeeded as expected as a team, but Trapp said he was proud the four players he mentioned all went on to solid NHL careers, and to wear Captain "C"s at the top level.

Obviously, as a coach, Trapp had to be an evaluator of talent. It was this area of expertise that would be most fully honed for the rest of Trapp's career. The NHL would come calling, and Trapp would head to the big league to work with Central Scouting. "I worked 10 years for the league. It was something to see the players coming up. It was a real learning experience," he said. He was told early on "that I was too tough on players because I was picking players that I'd want on my team. I had to learn to judge them on the talent they had."

There are players who Trapp recommended that he saw come up short of expectations, and others who exceeded his expectations. One player who achieved more than Trapp expected actually played for him—Kelly Buchberger. "I always believed he could make it, but he really came into his own in his last year of junior...He was a kid that just worked hard and persevered. He was just so determined he wasn't going to be denied." On the flip side was Jason Bonsignore, whom Trapp scouted in his NHL position. "I really thought this guy was going to be the next coming," he said of the 17-year-old. "But I learned some kids level off, and he did that at 17, and never got any better."

As a scout, Trapp soon found that what you saw on the ice wasn't enough to judge a hockey player's future. "The biggest part I learned as a scout was it's easy to judge the talent, but you've got to go see the kid play in tough situations. If I like a player I always want to see him on the road. I want to know if he plays the same way when he's down 9–1, as when he's up 9–1...You have to judge his character and mental toughness."

Trapp showed he had a nose for talent as he worked as a

scout, and Hockey Canada asked him to head up scouting to select Canada's World Junior team, a role he accepted and held for six years, starting in 1997. He points to his first year with the program as his most gratifying as the Canadian Junior team captured its fifth gold medal in a row.

Disappointment came later on Canadian soil. "The overtime loss to Russia in Winnipeg before that unbelievable crowd was a tough one," he said.

Win or lose, Trapp was always proud of the junior teams he was associated with. "Canada is such a class act. We'd get letters from hotels and tournament organizers about how good the players were to deal with. They are such great ambassadors for their country."

In some ways his position with Hockey Canada allowed Trapp to once again feel things for the game of hockey he'd sort of lost over the years. "I had lost sight of how passionate we [Canadians] are about the game," he said. "But I saw it again on my first trip into the Maritimes. The Maritimes people are just so passionate about the game." As he moved across Canada seeking out the best juniors, Trapp soon recognized again the passion this country has for hockey, and how ingrained is our desire to succeed at the top levels, such as the World Junior Championships.

Trapp often heard people suggesting the Canadian game had slipped a notch or two, but that is something he does not agree with. Granted, a decade ago Canada might have dominated international games more often, but the closeness of recent competitions is not due to Canadian slippage. "Our game hasn't slipped. It's just that countries below us have improved their game," he said, adding he believes that is particularly evident in the skills of European netminders. "That's been the biggest improvement. The level of play below us is so much better now."

However, the depth of talent in Canada was evident at the

2005 World Junior Championships, said Trapp. "This was an exceptional year. This may be the greatest World Junior team we've ever had. The depth was just so unbelievable."

Trapp said he was happy with his role with Hockey Canada and fully expected that he would finish out his career in the game there. Then along came the Toronto Maple Leafs. "They made me an unbelievable offer," said Trapp. He said several other NHL teams had made pitches for his services through the years, but the fit never felt quite right. The Toronto deal was different. "I thought it was a great thing to end up where I started," he said. "When I was a junior in Melville I belonged to Toronto, and now I'm back with them. It's coming full circle."

In fact, while John Ferguson Sr. first scouted Trapp to play in Melville, the circle is complete there as well, as he works for John Ferguson Jr. in Toronto now. "I was offered eight different jobs with NHL teams, but they weren't the right fit. This was the best thing that came along for me."

As Director of Amateur Scouting, Trapp leads a group that includes nearly a dozen full and part time scouts in Canada, the United States and Europe, and while he might head the group he still gets out and sees as much hockey as possible. He estimates he is on the road some 190 days a year, and sees around 200 games annually. "It used to be work eight months, get four off. Then it was work nine, get three off, now you really only get July. The draft is in June and the camps start in August," he said.

With the Leafs the goal is simple in preparing for the annual draft. "The way we work on it is we want the best player available," said Trapp. "If a goaltender is the best player available when it's our turn, we take the goaltender. We're just drafting talent."

Trapp fully expects to finish his career in the Leaf organization, hopefully taking less of a lead role within a few years. A part-time role would allow Trapp to do the one thing his scouting years have prevented: the opportunity to see family playing the game. "That's the toughest part, not being able to see the grandsons play," he said.

Hall of Fame?

Dream starts don't always have happy endings. Trevor Secundiak found that out when he was called into the coach's office with the Jacksonville Barracudas of the Atlantic Coast Hockey League (ACHL). "The coach called me in to his office [on a] Monday morning before a road trip and asked how I thought I was doing, and I told him exactly how I felt about the whole situation. He told me that they were going to release me," explained Secundiak in an email interview.

The news was a long way from the excitement Secundiak, who grew up in Yorkton, Saskatchewan, experienced in his first professional game in Florida. In his first game with the Barracudas against the Macon Trax, Secundiak netted what proved to be first goal in the reformed ACHL's history.

"We were on the power play. Their goalie came out to play it, and I kind of beat him to the puck. I just kind of turned and fired," he said in a Yorkton This Week article at the time. "It wasn't a very skillful goal. It was more luck than anything."

Luck or not, the goal quickly thrust Secundiak into the limelight. When he went to retrieve the puck from his first professional goal, he was told it was to be shipped to the Hockey Hall of Fame in Toronto. The next day when he arrived at the arena, he learned both his familiar #39 sweater and stick were also Hall of Fame bound.

"It's been kind of a crazy couple of days here," he said at the time. "There's been all kinds of people and friends calling."

Secundiak said he knew the goal was important to the league. In fact, he had a few side bets with golfing buddies that he would score the first goal. "That was my first thought, all the bets I had won with my golf buddies," he said with a laugh.

When he learned of the Hall of Fame, the goal took on greater meaning. "I realized it was the first league goal, but I didn't think it would be such a big wooha," he said. As for having his sweater, stick and puck in the Hall of Fame, Secundiak said he was naturally honoured. "It's very flattering," he said. "It's amazing how people work their whole careers to get into that place, and I score one goal and I get my name in there."

At the same time, Secundiak was pragmatic, noting it was only one goal, and in essence that goal was placed in the Hall of Fame even before it was scored. "I was just lucky enough to be the one that scored it," he said.

It was a storied start to his professional career, and early on things were going well as hockey came to the south. "Our first pro game was in Macon, Georgia. It was a good atmosphere, the fans there were really excited, they cheered for a shot on goal, a big check, and they even cheered when we iced the puck," said Secundiak in a November 17 email.

Admittedly Jacksonville was a long way from Yorkton, but fate sometimes plays a hand in a hockey career. Secundiak had looked as though he was headed to the college game, but inside information altered his course. "My thought process had a lot to do with feedback from other players such as Derek Allan, and Trevor Weisgerber, talking to guys that went to college on scholarships and they all said it was something that would take a lot of time, to get in the mix on teams," he said in November. "You might have to practice for a full year before you can play on the team, and that is something I did not want to have to do, I just wanted to play.

"So their feedback had a part of my decision. Also to see the world and to play in different places in the world was another big thing too, taking the same road trips for my 16 years of playing hockey in Yorkton got pretty boring as well."

Secundiak said the passing of his father also played a role in his decision to turn pro.

"Playing pro was more…fulfilling a dream…," he said. "A lot of it had to do with the passing of my father, me and him always talked about how perfect it would be to play hockey in Florida, and how convenient it would be that I am in the golf business as well. I never had the offer to play down here, two days after my dad died I got the call asking me if I would want to play pro hockey in Jacksonville Florida."

Certainly there was culture shock in heading to Florida, even if the game was still played on a sheet of ice. "Training camp here is a lot different," he said in November. "There were only 30 guys in camp and all range in age, some guys already have contracts signed.

"It was really competitive; the same guys were always on the ice together, there were no different ice sessions, so you came really close to being a team in camp. You also got concerned when a guy got cut and where he was going afterwards, because it might be able to help you if you got released.

"There was a lot more pressure to make the team here, because this is it, and if you don't make it now you have to pack up and take a journey somewhere else or head back home. And that journey could take you across the country."

Secundiak made it through the trial of fire that was his first professional training camp, but he still had to adapt to a game a step up from his junior experience in the Saskatchewan Junior Hockey League.

"As for playing against other pro hockey players it was a lot more physical than junior, and quicker," he said in November. "The players down here are a lot smarter without the puck. And it was very emotional for me cause I knew if my Dad was alive he would have been there. Then I scored the first goal of the league, and heard about what was going to happen about the Hall of Fame, it was hard to hold back the tears."

With the big goal history, Secundiak began to settle into life as a hockey player in Florida, which was different from playing the game amid a Saskatchewan winter. "It's very difficult to focus because there is so much to see and do," he said in early December. "All the golf courses are still open and a guy always wants to play, and there are all kinds of attractions and shops and amusement parks and beaches.

"A lot of us young kids pass this fun stuff up just so we can stay down here and play. Sure there will be days off where we can do this kind of stuff, but there are a lot of times where we will go to the gym instead of going to the beach or to play golf.

"We have pretty much learned that this is not a vacation—we are here to work and win a championship."

Interest in the Barracudas helped keep the players focused on the ice. "My first impressions of the city itself were that the people that got involved with the hockey team were really good; community involvement is really picking up," he said in November. "People are now starting to see that there is pro hockey in town and are getting interested.

"As to calling it a hockey town—probably not, especially coming close to the New Year with all of the college football here. We are right in between the Florida State Seminoles and the Florida Gators in regards to location, and they're both about a 45 minute drive, so it's really tough to be a hockey town with the football, NASCAR, and National Football League.

"Right now we are probably on page 5 of the sports."

Still, by mid-December 2003, Secundiak said the team and the league were drawing more attention.

"Things have really picked up with us getting noticed," he said. "We are on the nightly news, and we get write-ups in the paper. We will go around town and people will see our jackets and come and talk to us, ask for an autograph, but a team still has to win to get noticed, because there are a lot of other things down here in the sports world that a team can disappear very quickly."

The good news for the team was that it improved as the young season progressed. "The team started off slow but we had a good month of November, so we are sitting in a playoff spot right now," he said. "The guys are starting to gel on the ice and we are starting to connect well."

Still, interest in hockey tended to stop at the local team, with hockey outside of the league a virtual unknown in Jacksonville. "People don't talk about the NHL down here very much," he said in December. "Like right now, I couldn't even tell you who is hurt or who is playing well, or what team is in first place; we see some coverage but not like you see on TSN. College sports and NASCAR racing seem to be dominant along with the NFL of course."

Initially though, Secundiak's stock appeared to be improving as the team itself did. "My season started out good, I scored a bit in the first 10 games, but now I am playing a bit of a checking role, shutting down other teams' top lines, more of a spark plug role like I did when I first played in Yorkton for Klipper (Wade

Klippenstein)," he said in the December 17 interview. "Still, I'm on the power play, playing defence like I did with the Terriers.

"But I think I have to start scoring a little more on the power play."

Secundiak's desire to score more often would prove prophetic in the coming weeks. "What was going on here for the whole month of December kind of turned me off from being here," he said in Sunday's email interview. "I talked to the coach about my role on the team and he told me that I had to play a defensive role on the team, and shut down opposing teams' top lines. This was something that I took in and did for him.

"I really did not like that role because I wanted to score and be a lot more offensive, and playing defence really took away my keys to being a good player, which is my speed and stick handling ability."

As the sting of being cut eased, Secundiak said he has taken the move in stride. "My feelings about it are that I am really excited about coming home," he said. "I have no regrets about my decision to come here; it just was not my time yet. I made a lot of friends and lived this experience to the fullest. I had a taste of pro hockey, and realized that if a coach wants you to be someone or something on the ice, as tough as it is, you've got to be that type of player.

"It's just finding the team that can match the player's role without making drastic changes to his lineup."

On many levels Secundiak knew the cut was coming. "Like I said, it was almost like a relief packing up the gear, because I knew that I would not be back here to do something I really wasn't enjoying," he said. "I enjoy playing hockey, and I am a very coachable kid. For me it was not if I get released my career is over, it was just pick up and move on.

"Obviously things were not working, so it was for the better. I said my good-byes to the team and friends. But I look at it as hey, what can we accomplish next?"

Still Reaching for the Brass Ring

Brian Propp can look back on a long National Hockey League career with pride, and a knowledge that coming close is sometimes as good as it gets. Propp would play 1,016 regular season games in the NHL, and record more than 1,004 points, stellar numbers by any standards, and a career really prefaced by his rookie year.

Propp joined the Philadelphia Flyers as a rookie for the 1979-80 season, and proceeded to be part of the team that ran off an incredible 35-game undefeated streak, an NHL record. "That was something that was almost magical. We just got on a roll," said Propp.

As he looks back Propp recognizes the Flyers at that time were a talented crew, including the likes of linemates Bobby Clarke and Reggie Leach, who helped the rookie left winger record an assist on the game-winning goal in his first NHL contest. "It was against the New York Islanders and it was in the third period and it was the eventual winner. It was against [netminder] Billy Smith," he recalled.

By season's end, Propp would establish a new team record for rookie scoring with 34 goals and 75 points, a mark since eclipsed by Dave Poulin and Mikael Renberg. In spite of his torrid scoring, Propp would miss out on the Calder Cup as NHL rookie of the year to a defenceman in Boston named Ray Bourque.

But the undefeated streak went beyond goals and assists. Propp said it was a time when everything simply fell into place for the team. "I think it started with coaching. Pat Quinn was very good at Xs and Os, and systems.

"And, we had a very balanced team, with four strong lines. Everybody had a role and played it well. Different guys were coming up big whenever we needed them to do it."

The Flyers were backstopped in net by the tandem of Phil Myre and Pete Peeters; solid, but not exceptional netminders at the time, but Propp said they fit the mold of the team on its streak. "It was just the type of teamwork we had that year. They didn't always have to come up big the way the team played in front of them."

The Flyers would ride the streak into a strong playoff run, propelling Propp to the Stanley Cup finals in his rookie season. It would be the first of five finals for Propp, three with the Flyers and one each with Boston and Minnesota, but there would be no ring. "Unfortunately I was never on the champagne drinking side of it," he said.

However, while he came up a goal or two short of the Cup victory through the years, Propp said he doesn't look at it as a major failing in his pro career. Instead, he takes pride in being there in the finals as often as he was. "It's very difficult just to get to the finals," he said. As he looks back he remains in the top-25 in just about every finals statistical column. Altogether he played in 160 playoff games and contributed 148 points.

For Propp a career is not just about Stanley Cup rings, although they are a goal while playing. In retirement though, one needs to look at the overall career. "You just have to look at what you've done, and how you played. If you gave 100 per cent every game, and contributed, you can be proud of that."

One thing no one can argue with is Propp's contribution to his teams over the years. In 10 seasons as a Flyer, the left wing with his familiar wrist shot tallied 40 or more goals four times, 40 or more assists nine times, and 90 or more points four times. His total of 849 points as a Flyer places him third on the team's all-time list behind Hockey Hall of Famers Bobby Clarke and Bill Barber. He also ranked third on the club's all-time points list, and is second on the Flyers' all-time list in goals, 369, and assists, 480. For his outstanding play he has been inducted into the Flyers' Hall of Fame.

For many of those goals Propp showed a flair for exciting the fans with his post-red light celebrations which became known simply as the "Guffaw." "The year was 1986 when I decided that I wanted to show a little more personality and excitement after I scored goals... Tim Kerr was in the midst of his scoring prowess of scoring 50 plus goals for four years straight and his reaction was low key and matter of fact after he scored. I wanted to try something different, but wasn't sure what it would be.

"I've always spent some time in Ocean City, New Jersey, in the summer and one of my best friends, Scott McKay, was a lifeguard for the OCBP. We did a lot of things together and we decided in the summer of 1986 to go to a Howie Mandel show at one of the Casinos. Howie Mandel is a very famous Canadian comedian and they discovered the "Guffaw" at his show. Howie asked the crowd if they would like to mess up the next comedian that came to town. Of course, everyone said yes. He showed the crowd how to do the "Guffaw." He did the "Guffaw" movement with his right arm. He started with a short left to right wave followed by extending his arm straight up to the ceiling. This was called the "Guffaw."

"I'll never forget my first goal at the start of the 1986–87 season. I was thinking about the "Guffaw" and finally scored my first of the year. I had the usual crowd of players congratulating me after the goal. Then, as I broke away from the pack and headed to centre ice, I put my right glove under my left arm and did the "Guffaw" as I skated toward center ice. I have always said the word guffaw as I was doing it. I had finally done the "Guffaw"...I finally had my signature mark after scoring, which showed my personality on the ice...

"Howie Mandel heard about the "Guffaw" at the end of the 1986–87 season and I got a call from him in the Flyers dressing room before a playoff game against the Rangers. I thought Turk, the equipment manager, was playing a joke, but sure enough, it was Howie Mandel on the line. He thought it was great that I was using the "Guffaw" and didn't mind if I used it. That was a thrill for me to get his approval. Since that phone call, I have been at Howie's show in Atlantic City a number of times and had a chance to visit with him after the show. We get a good laugh about the "Guffaw" and I'm sure we will for many years to come."

Propp would play for four other teams, but will be best remembered as a Flyer, and the "Guffaw" was his trademark as he continued on his NHL career.

It was fitting his final NHL goal would come at the Spectrum in Philly. "It was my 1000th point. It was an afternoon game and I had a ton of people at the game," said the then member of the Hartford Whalers.

Propp's contributions to a team's success goes back further than his NHL days. Born in Lanigan, he grew up at Neudorf, Saskatchewan, where hockey was simply part of the community fabric each winter. He said playing as a youngster in a small Prairie town was a great way to learn the game. "We could just scrape together enough to have a team, so I was playing on two or three different teams, often with a lot older kids," he said.

However, while he was playing lots of hockey, he admitted he had no NHL dreams at a young age. "I never really thought about it. I was just a small farm boy, just enjoying myself, having fun playing the game," he said.

Then in his Bantam year he was picked up by a Yorkton-Melville team heading to the Wrigley Tournament in Oshawa, Ontario, and he said he finally began to realize he might go somewhere beyond his home town thanks to hockey. Propp played with the Melville Millionaires of the Saskatchewan Junior Hockey League and set a scoring record with 168 points as a 15-year-old. "That was a telling point for me too," he said.

The next season Propp moved up to the Brandon Wheat Kings of the Western Hockey League, and again had immediate impact. He was third in league scoring in his rookie season with 135 points. In his next two seasons he would improve on that total with 182 and 194 points, both league-leading totals.

Of course the Wheat Kings of the era, 1976–79, were a powerhouse as a team, with such players as Bill Derlago, Laurie Boschman, Brad McCrimmon, Dave Semenko and Glen Hanlon on board. "We had a very, very powerful team," said Propp. "There were a bunch of guys that became NHL players that played for a long time." As a result, in the years Propp played in Brandon the team lost only 12, eight and five regular season games.

Yet in the WHL the top prize would elude Propp too. In his final year Brandon did make it to the Memorial Cup final against Peterborough, and while one of the best finals ever, it would be the Petes on top, not the Wheat Kings. "We lost in triple overtime—one goal either way—but we were right there."

The score ended 2–1, with Propp scoring the lone Brandon marker. "I needed to score another," he said.

"It was a very memorable game. A lot of people still talk about it—but it was pretty disappointing too."

Certainly Propp's WHL career is still talked about, and well-remembered. In fact, in May 1999, he was named the greatest left wing in the history of the Canadian Hockey League as chosen by a panel of journalists, CHL officials and league historians.

While the big trophies always seemed a goal or two out of Propp's grasp, it all fell into place for him on the international stage in 1987, as he was selected to Team Canada for the Canada Cup. Propp lined up with two of the greatest players the game has seen, Wayne Gretzky and Mario Lemieux. He said the line was one "I was sort of expecting," especially with his Philadelphia Flyers coach Mike Keenan at the helm. "I took on a lot more of a defensive role, and let those guys handle the puck," he said with a chuckle. He added adjusting to the two talented linemates wasn't that difficult. "When you're an NHL player of that calibre you're able to adjust to any player you are put with," he said.

The Canada Cup would be captured by Canada that year, and for Propp it was a chance to finally feel the exhilaration of a finals win, something that had eluded him in the Stanley Cup hunt. In fact, that very same year Propp set the Flyer record for most points in a playoff year when he recorded 28 points in 26 games as the team advanced to the 1987 Stanley Cup Finals. "To be on the winning side of the Canada Cup I was finally getting a taste of that feeling," he said. Playing on Team Canada also gave Propp "some of the best hockey I ever played. It was tremendous hockey."

On two other occasions Propp skated with Canadian colours at World Championships, something he stills looks upon as an honour. "Anytime you can represent your country, you'd have to be an idiot to turn that down," he said. "It's your opportunity to contribute to your country."

Back in his home province, Propp's career has been recognized with his induction into the Saskatchewan Sports Hall of Fame. Now, after retiring from the NHL in 1994, he waits in hopes of a call from the Hockey Hall of Fame one day. He said he felt a taste of what it must be like to be inducted when he was selected the best left winger in the history of Canadian junior hockey, and he would like to take that final step. He said he believes he deserves to be there. "I think the stats are there to back it up." For example, he is plus-300 on his career, a testament to defence too.

Upon retirement Propp remained involved in the game, first starting a hockey arena in Jersey, where he said interest in the game grows with the availability of ice. "It was a good challenge, and I was very satisfied with the results."

He moved on to work with Philadelphia Flyer radio for a number of years.

Propp said he also finds time to work at the occasional hockey school or camp. "It's fun seeing the improvement. It really makes it all worthwhile."

The next generation of Propps is also on the ice with both daughter Paige and son Jackson on the same Mite team.

A World of Coaching

Kelly Lovering self-admittedly was never a great hockey player, but he developed insights into the game that would take him around the world as a coach. "I'm your basic example of a guy who cares for the game, and the game just keeps pushing me along," he said. "It's taken me around the world."

The globe trotting started when he learned to play the game as a kid growing up in Regina. "I was like everybody else way back in the '60s: I played the game," but he added that while he was in the Regina Pats organization, he never climbed to its upper echelons. "I played one year at the University of Manitoba, but it wasn't much of a program back then. Playing on the team then doesn't mean as much as it would now."

While a career as a player was out of reach, Lovering, who became a teacher by profession, soon found he had something to give the game as a teacher on the ice, too. His teaching certificate would include stints at Campbell Collegiate in Regina, and at the famed Notre Dame College in Wilcox, two stops that saw him blossom as a coach as well.

Through his years as a school teacher and coach, Lovering's resume of success began to build. As a coach or manager he captured provincial titles in rugby, football, basketball and at every level of hockey starting at Pee Wee, through Bantam, Midget, the now-extinct Juvenile division, and finally at the Junior level with the Notre Dame Hounds in 1988. In total Lovering won 14 provincial championships.

The Centennial Cup-winning Hounds playing in their first season in the Saskatchewan Junior Hockey League holds a special place in Lovering's heart. "It was a very good hockey team. There were a lot of great guys on that team."

One player who sticks out for Lovering is goaltender Curtis Joseph, who went on to star in the National Hockey League. "Joseph was going to quit hockey," said Lovering, who recalled the young Ontario netminder seeking help to find an American college team to play for.

Lovering asked Joseph how good he was, and the netminder replied, "I'm really good but nobody knows it."

Lovering arranged for a scout to take a look at Joseph, but the scout settled on the opposition netminder that night, another future NHLer, Mike Dunham. Joseph called again and said he hadn't heard anything and that he might as well quit the game. Fortunately for hockey, Lovering convinced him to join the Hounds.

"I said, 'we're starting a Junior A team, why don't you come out here and see what happens'." As it turned out Joseph back-stopped the team to a national championship, and that opened doors all the way to the NHL. "He had a lot of private things to fight through as kid that nobody needs to know about, but he got over it all," said Lovering. Joseph was special because he believed in himself.

The national crown with the Hounds was one of four Lovering would be involved with on some level.

His decade at Notre Dame, from 1980 through 1990, was in many ways the program's golden years on the ice. It was enough to bring Lovering to the attention of Hockey Canada. They liked his combination of teaching and coaching, and hired Lovering to coordinate and have input into coaching manuals which are used at all levels of hockey across the country. The job soon expanded to giving clinics as well.

When the International Ice Hockey Federation came looking for someone to help get the game going in fledgling hockey countries such as the Netherlands, South Africa, New Zealand, China and Australia the nod went to Lovering to pack his hockey manuals and board planes for the exotic hockey locales.

In some countries the experience was a culture shock in terms of just what hockey means, and in how it is played. For example, China, which has since pared back its hockey program to concentrate on sports such as speed skating and diving, was a challenge when he toured giving clinics in 1986. The country was moving from Group "C" to Group "B" on the international level, and they needed someone who could go over and help them prepare for hockey at the higher level.

Lovering said it was not quite hockey as Canadians enjoy it. He recalled one game where instead of glass there was only netting. "People would stick their faces right up to the mesh," he said. He often wondered how many stitches fans went home with after a game. In another rink "people would start fires in the stands to keep warm. By the third period you couldn't even see the ice," he said.

While fans showed up, they knew nothing of the game. During warm-ups the fans would cheer whenever the Chinese team scored on their own goaltender, and jeer when the opposition put one past theirs, said Lovering. He also recalls seeing one player hitting the ice wearing one hockey skate and one speed skate. "He could really turn that one way," he said with a laugh. "But you could still see the passion for the game."

At times the passion was almost scary. Lovering said in one instance he saw a player skating on a pond and broke through the ice. When he crawled out, he realized he'd lost his hockey glove. "He went back in and came back out with it."

It was different in places such as South Africa, New Zealand and Australia. "In those places expatriate Canadians supply the impetus for the game," said Lovering.

In Australia, where Lovering would spend four years as national team coach starting in 1998, "They've had hockey since 1908. That was because Canadian ships would land, and get something going." Today though, hockey is growing by leaps and bounds Down Under. "Their national league has eight teams now, and there are four new rinks in the last year," said Lovering. Four rinks may not sound like a lot, but in 1998, when Lovering arrived in the country, there were only four rinks in the whole country.

The opportunity to develop a sport he loved in a country just taking to the game attracted Lovering to move to Australia, as did an opportunity to coach his son Tyler, something he has never done before. "He was playing senior hockey in Avonlea and Rouleau when an old Hound of mine asked him to play for the Sydney Bears. He went in '93, and never returned except to visit." Lovering would coach his son in the World Championships all four years, winning one silver and three bronze medals. Tyler has continued to play for Australia in 2002, '03 and '04, getting another bronze in 2004.

While the sport was growing in Australia, expectations for the sport were different than you would see in Canada. In 1998, Lovering coached the Australian National team to its first medal at the World "C" Championship in decades, taking silver, one of four medals on the international scene he would earn in his career. "I'm crying because we didn't get the gold and the team is cheering they got silver. There were two guys from Canada, and me, and we're crying over the loss," he said. "We lost to Bulgaria 5–4 in overtime. I'm telling them that's how close they were to being World Champions."

Lovering would guide the Aussie team to two silvers and a bronze, but after four years of helping a sport take flight, he'd had enough. "You really end up coaching over there," said Lovering. "...You'd go there with these beautiful practice plans, and it was no use giving them the drills because out of 25 guys you might have some good players, because they were ex-Canadians, and some who could barely skate."

It was a case of suspending much of what years in the Canadian game had taught Lovering. "I had to tell myself, 'I'm not in Canada anymore. This is not my grandson's team playing. It's just a bunch of guys who love the game and want to play'." Even the parents in the stands needed to be taught the game.

Although there was a challenge to dealing with novices at every level and aspect of the game, Lovering said working with Australian youth also had its rewards. He recalled one balance drill where he had youngsters jumping over pylons on their skates. "A mom yelled to her son and asked 'how did you do that?' The youngster pointed to me and said 'because that man said I could'," said Lovering.

At the national level Lovering said there was a layer of cream, but it was not a thick layer. "I could pull 25 guys out of the system who could really play, but the problem was we didn't have another 25 quality guys to play against."

Still, Lovering sees Australia as a place hockey will put down deep roots. "They love the game. I could charge $5 for people to watch my practices for the national team…I would think they're the best team in the Southern Hemisphere."

The Australian developmental system works well for a new sport, mimicking rugby teams, where a team has clubs from beginner to the elite national league, so all the players learn the same system. "The only thing you have to do is leave enough freedom and risk taking for people to use their talents," he said.

In talking of the Aussie team, Lovering still used terms like "my" and "our" three years after leaving the program, indicating a deep tie to the game Down Under. However, he still points to Notre Dame as his most memorable time involved with the game. "You never get Notre Dame out of your heart. Notre Dame gets ingrained pretty deeply into your whole being."

When Lovering did leave the Australian program, partly because of the pressures of running a hockey program from beginner to national team and in part because "we missed winter," he returned to Canada thinking of relaxing. Lovering was soon behind the bench of the SJHL Estevan Bruins, a return to a league that had included both his Notre Dame days, and a shortened season as the first-ever coach of the expansion LaRonge Ice Wolves.

The LaRonge experience was unique, given the team struggled as a new franchise. "It was my first time losing 16 games in a row," said Lovering. It was also rewarding "having the guys come off the ice after a loss and wanting to play the next game.

"As a coach, if the minute your kids leave the ice they want to get right back on for the next game, then you've done your job."

In Estevan, Lovering said he was simply out of energy, so he retired, expecting to be done with hockey. A hockey clinic in Notre Dame changed that. Sarah Howald, coach of the University of Regina women's team, attended the clinic. "She asked 'why don't you just mentor us? You don't have to jump in with both feet'."

Now he's back on the bench helping as much as he can, adding every win by the girls is a new highlight for him. "Sometimes I just seem to get carried along in a wave of things," said Lovering of his ever-evolving career in the game. "... There's a lot of good things the game has given me. I just hope before I die I can give it back."

Making Tough Choices

Like many youngsters growing up through the 1950s in Saskatchewan, Cliff Koroll dreamed of playing in the National Hockey League. With that dream came more dreams, those of one day hoisting the Stanley Cup.

In the spring of 1971, as a member of the Chicago Black Hawks Koroll was fulfilling his first dream and appeared on the verge of completing the second. "In 1970–71 we played the Montreal Canadiens in the finals. We were up three games to two going into Montreal, and we were leading by a goal going into the third period, and they came back to beat us in the game," recalled Koroll. He said it was a case where Pete Mahovlich had his stick around the throat of Hawks defenceman Keith Magnuson, which allowed him to get the puck and make a pass that ended in a goal for Montreal. "And, there was no call on it [the hook]."

The Canadiens win sent the series back to the fabled Chicago Stadium, and again the Hawks took the lead. "We were up 2–0 in the middle of the second period," said Koroll. Bobby

Hull would take a patented slapshot that rang off the crossbar. The puck bounced out and Montreal made a long clearing shot as both teams switched up players. Somehow Tony Esposito in the Hawk net misplayed the dump-in and Montreal was given life. Henri Richard would then score the tying, and winning goals, and the Stanley Cup dream for that season was dead. "I still wake up nights from that one. It was so close I could taste the champagne. It was very, very disappointing," said Koroll.

The Hawks would be back in the 1973 Stanley Cup finals, losing this time in six games to Montreal, "so I'm not a very big Montreal fan," he said.

While Koroll would play a total of 11 seasons in the NHL, all with Chicago, he never came closer to a Cup. "That's the one void in my life. I was very fortunate to play the game. I have a great wife and family. The one thing that still bugs me is not winning the Stanley Cup. The '71 series, it just won't go away."

Still, Koroll looks at his career in the game with pride, realizing his road to an NHL career was not necessarily typical of his era. Born in Canora, Saskatchewan, he grew up in Saskatoon, where he started skating at three but played very little organized hockey as a youth.

"I had three older brothers. They always built a rink in the backyard, a little strip in the garden," he said, adding that was only one of several skating options. "Within a four block radius of our house there were eight outdoor rinks.

Koroll's three older brothers, Bill, Ron and the late Bruce Koroll, were all huge influences on his life. "They always took me to the park to play hockey, or to toss a football or play catch. They never even once hesitated. They were always there to support me, even through my pro career."

As a youngster Koroll made repeated use of those skating options too. "If it was 30, 40 below, you never thought about it.

You'd come back with frozen hands, feet, cheeks, ear lobes, but you played. I don't know if it was ignorance, or just a love of the game. But all my friends did it. If we weren't playing hockey on the rinks, we played shinny on the street, shooting frozen horse apples after the milk cart went by. "We didn't have organized hockey until we were 10 years old."

When organized hockey did start, it was slightly different in nature than what is familiar today. Koroll said there were six teams, one after each of the NHL teams of the era, all sponsored by the Kinsmen Club. "We played one game a week, every Friday night in the arena, one of only two indoor facilities in the whole city."

The opportunity to play in those games was also something players had to earn. Koroll said each player had a citizenship card he had to have signed by four people each week. The people rated the youngsters as good, fair or unsatisfactory. One unsatisfactory and you didn't play. Two fairs and you didn't play.

"It had to be signed by your school teacher, so you had to do well in school. It had to be signed by your Sunday school teacher, so you had to attend church, you couldn't sleep in on Sunday. One of your parents had to sign it, so you had to do your housework. And, one of the Kinsmen Club had to sign it at the rink, so you couldn't goof around and get in trouble at the rink." It was a system Koroll said helped develop a person beyond the game, but one which wouldn't work today. But in those days kids worked hard to play every game with a season that had only 15 games, followed by playoffs. "It boggles my mind, kids today playing 60–70 games a year," he said.

Koroll said he believes he benefited from fewer games. "Practice is what gets you there, not the games." He said all the time on outdoor rinks practicing the skating, the shooting and learning the game was what took him to the next level.

For Koroll the next level was a successful one. At 15, in his first year playing Midget hockey, he won a provincial championship. The next year, moving up to Juvenile, he again helped take a provincial banner.

The next season, at 17, Koroll made a decision many thought was disastrous, but one he said put the finishing touches on him as a hockey player capable of playing in the NHL. While most talented youngsters headed to junior in Canada, Koroll chose to accept a hockey scholarship at the University of Denver. "It was not the thing to do. In that day nobody made it to the NHL from college hockey," he said.

However, Koroll said his brothers pushed him toward securing an education, and when Denver coach Murray Armstrong offered the scholly, it was an easy decision. "They had a history of being an excellent program."

Koroll might have seen the merit in college hockey, but most others didn't. "All the media in Saskatoon really knocked me down. They said by choosing college I didn't stand a chance of making the NHL because [I] was going to become a scholar."

While Saskatoon hockey pundits questioned the move, Koroll said he learned he had to step up his hockey quickly in college. "There were guys on our team that were 27-year-old seniors. Talk about growing up fast, playing against men when you're still a growing boy," he said.

Under the tutelage of Armstrong, Koroll said he matured as a player. "He [Armstrong] was probably one of the most influential people in my life, other than my brothers and family," he said. "...He was a great motivator. He could get you to run through that wall...I have a tremendous amount of respect for him. He was not just a great coach, but a tremendous person." It was Armstrong who fortified Koroll's NHL dream too. "He always told me 'you're going to play in the National Hockey League. If you want it bad enough you'll get it'."

In his freshman year, Koroll played only on the varsity team, but practiced, again learning through the process. "We practiced for three hours a day."

In his sophomore year, Koroll began to enjoy success in Denver. "We should have won the National Championship that year. We were playing in Minneapolis. I scored a goal everybody in the arena saw except the referee and the goal judge; I even have a picture of the puck bulging the net." But the goal was not allowed. "One of our guys argued too much and took a penalty." The ensuing power play goal sank the Denver squad.

In his junior year it was close again. "We lost to the University of North Dakota in double overtime to go to the National Championship," said Koroll. "North Dakota went on to win it, so had we won that game we'd have probably won the championship too."

That left Koroll's senior year, a season that turned around with a huge loss. The team was playing in an international tournament in Colorado Springs against teams from Japan, Finland and the Soviet Union. They met the Soviets in the final "and they trounced us 8–2.

"But we never lost another game that year. We won 26 in a row to win the National Championship…It was one of the biggest thrills of my career."

With his college career ending on a career high, Koroll was faced with the decision of what was next.

A baseball player as well, having returned to Saskatchewan each summer to play in the Northern Saskatchewan Baseball League, Koroll was offered a tryout with the Minnesota Twins farm club in Denver, managed at the time by the famous Billy Martin. "They offered me a contract to play baseball," he said. The $5,000-a-year deal was one of three options he had to consider.

Koroll also had an offer to teach and coach hockey in Eastern Canada for $6,500 a year.

"And the Black Hawks offered me $8,000, so I went for the money," he joked.

The first season in the pros was spent with the Hawks' farm club in Dallas. "We won the Central League Championship," said Koroll, adding that became his calling card for a real shot at sticking in Chicago the next season, since the parent club was rebuilding after a last-place finish.

Koroll said his first game in Chicago was awe-inspiring. "I sat in a locker room between [Tony] Esposito and Stan Mikita, and Bobby Hull was right across from me. I grew up idolizing guys like Mikita and Hull and there I was in the same locker room," he said. "...My first game I was afraid, and I was nervous. The noise in that building [the Stadium] was just deafening."

Koroll's first goal came while playing four-on-four against the New York Rangers. With a player short on both teams Hawks coach Billy Reay sent out three Saskatchewan rookies, long-time friend Keith Magnuson on defence, Koroll, and Jim Wiste at forward. "Jim and I looked at each other, 'what are we doing out here?'" said Koroll. But it was a Wiste feed that set up Koroll to beat Ed Giacomin for his first goal, the first of 208 regular season goals, to go with 254 assists.

At home in Chicago, he scored a hat trick two games later, and the line of Koroll, Wiste and Stan Mikita was set for the season. "I played on a line with Stan Mikita. I played with him for 10 years. He kind of took me under his wing and helped me. We were roommates on the road for 10 years too," he said, adding "people don't really know how good he [Mikita] was in all facets of the game. They know he could score goals, but he was as good a defensive player as there was in the league."

As close as Mikita and Koroll became, Keith Magnuson and Koroll seemed connected by kismet. The pair grew up in Saskatoon together, and played in Denver as teammates, before again both moving on to Chicago. The duo retired the same year, with Magnuson becoming the Hawks coach, and Koroll his assistant. Even after that Magnuson would become president of the team's alumni and Koroll the vice president. "We were very, very close," he said.

Being so close, Koroll said Magnuson's death in a car accident in 2003 was very difficult. "He was not the most skilled player, but he sure made up for it with the size of his heart...He was tough. He wouldn't back down from anyone."

Although the lack of a Stanley Cup ring still haunts Koroll, he said he is satisfied with his choices throughout his career, and after. Today he works with Cargill, following 21 years with the Hawks, including seven years as coach, and two in the head office after retiring in 1980. He and his wife Lynnae have three children, Jason, C.J. and Amanda, all now grown.

From Hockey to Lacrosse and Back

Justin Keller pulled off a unique double as a junior athlete, topping the Saskatchewan Box Lacrosse League in scoring in 2003, and then turning to hockey to lead the Saskatchewan Junior Hockey League in scoring through its 2003–04 regular season. It was an interesting scenario for a Canadian, topping scoring in both of this country's national sports—lacrosse being our national summer sport and hockey our winter one.

In the lacrosse league, Keller, as a member of the Yorkton Bulldogs, scored 53 goals and 42 assists for 95 points in only 12 games, or an average of 7.92 points per game. The 95 points were 16 better than runner-up and long-time lacrosse teammate Chris Lesanko. Then in the SJHL he scored 42 goals and 56 assists in 60 games, to become the first member of the Yorkton Terriers to win the scoring crown.

While Keller looks back on both scoring titles with pride, he admits the hockey crown is the one he cherishes the most. "For sure the hockey. It doesn't compare to anything else. It was always my main goal to focus on my hockey," he said. "Lacrosse was something fun for a month. It was more for conditioning in my mind. That was the way I was looking at it."

In that respect box lacrosse is a great off-season activity for hockey players. "You're using all the same skills except not wearing skates out there," he said. "And the mental part of the game is similar. It really helps when you're jumping into hockey."

Having a good run in lacrosse helped put his mind back in focus for hockey. "It's good to play lacrosse and get your mind off things," he said. "It makes you feel good about the summer and will get me in a good frame of mind for when I start to play hockey again."

In many ways the conditioning afforded Keller by his success in lacrosse helped set the stage for his success scoring in the SJHL in the following season. It turned out to be a season he keenly recalls. "It felt really good, but there was a lot of pressure throughout the year. People were talking about it, but I just tried not to think about it too much," he said.

At the same time Keller said he was only human, and found himself checking the stats to see how he was doing. "It was kind of tough, but at the end of the day it's all about your team," he said. "If the team is doing well everything falls into place."

While Keller was the one getting his name in the record books, no one wins a scoring title alone. "I have to give my teammates a lot of the credit too, and Ches and Eddie (coaches Don Chesney and Ed Zawatsky) for giving me the chance to play my game," he said.

Twelve games into the SJHL season Keller had eight goals and 11 assists. With the 19 points on the season he was tied for second in league scoring—three points back of league-leading Simon Nadeau of Humboldt with 22 points. He was named Player of the Week for October 13 in the league. "I want to try and put up some big numbers," he said at the time. On nights he had scored one goal, he would have liked to have netted a second or third. "I've set out some goals, to go out and score as many goals as I can," he said, adding that winning is still the key goal. "You get personal success when the team is doing well."

By the all-star game, Keller was an obvious selection to the Sherwood Conference roster. Keller sat with 37 goals and 47 assists for 78 points, tops in the league, and poised to take the scoring title.

While lacrosse was an option for Keller to consider once he turned pro, hockey was always first in Keller's heart, so it was no surprise he signed a contract in the summer of 2004 to join the Lubbock Cotton Kings of the Central Hockey League.

For Keller, the Cotton Kings became the team of choice based on the likelihood of greater ice time with the CHL franchise. "I think it came down to looking at my options, at all the teams I had talked to this summer, and deciding what was the best fit for me," he said in an interview shortly after the deal was inked. Lubbock was a good fit in the sense the Cotton Kings are in a rebuilding mode, with a new coach at the helm. "So there's a greater chance for me to play," said Keller.

With the contract finally inked the 6-foot, 190-pound Keller said, "It's kind of nice, there's no pressure right now."

At the same time the decision didn't come easily. "For awhile I was talking to a lot of teams, then it got down to about four teams, and the last couple of weeks three," he said. There were a couple of other teams he was leaning toward, but Lubbock ended up the choice.

Keller said his stint in the Western Hockey League, before coming to the Terriers part-way through the 2002–03 season, helped push him toward the Cotton Kings. In the WHL Keller was shuffled around, and never had a lot of opportunity to just play his own game. "That kind of helped my decision...Not playing so much up there (in the WHL) didn't really help me develop," he said. He credits the Terriers with giving him the chance to show his skills. "They let me play my game all the way and that got my confidence up."

In talking to Lubbock rookie coach Chris Dashney, Keller said he had been told he'd be given the opportunity to do his thing as a Cotton King. "He told me I'll be given a great opportunity to play, and to fit in," he said. "...He said he'd give me an opportunity to go down there and fit into the top two lines."

The trip south would reunite Keller with Jason Beatty, both Sturgis-area products who played minor hockey together as well as the last season-and-a-half as Terriers. Although not something that factored into the decision-making process, Keller admitted having a familiar face on a journey into Texas hockey would be great. "It's nice going somewhere that far away and knowing someone else on the team so well," he said.

Keller said the scoring crown was a definite door opener as he began looking for pro hockey options with his junior career complete. "I didn't think about it much at the time, but all those sort of things really help. Pro coaches really don't get a chance to see you play, so they hear about you by word-of-mouth, and then go on the Internet and check out your stats," he said.

As for his prowess scoring on the lacrosse floor, Keller was a force from the first time the Yorkton Bulldogs stepped on the cement as an expansion franchise in the Saskatchewan league. The hot hand around the net was the result of a simple philosophy of going to the net and getting shots, a key to box lacrosse when double digit scorers and 50 shots a night are the norm. "I'm getting a lot of shots on net. I don't know how many," said Keller early in the 2003 lacrosse season. "It helps when you shoot, you score."

Used to the field lacrosse game, Keller did note the nets in box are a smaller target. "It's a little tougher to score because the nets are smaller compared to field," he observed. While the nets might be smaller, Keller zeroed in on how to get the ball into the mesh, and ended up leading the league in scoring. Asked if a scoring title was a goal, Keller was quick to say no. "That's not important to me at all," he said early in the year. "As long as the team is doing good. As long as we're succeeding as a team I'm happy... We're trying to be the number one team in the league."

"If it happens at the end of the year, it happens," said Keller, adding he didn't want to think of scoring titles. "It takes your mind off things. You can get selfish. You can get a little preoccupied," he said.

Offensively, it helped to have a familiar face feeding you the ball, and that is what Keller had in teammate Chris Lesanko. "We've played together on the same line on attack ever since we started. It's always been me and him," said Keller. "He's always been the kind of guy who's a playmaker to set up guys."

On the floor, Keller said the key is staying focused on what is happening. "You've always got to have your head on a swivel," he said. "You've got to keep your mind focused. You've always got to be thinking out there."

On offense, while being a clear go-to guy on the Bulldogs to get shots, Keller also at times took on the role of quarterbacking the offensive unit. That often meant slowing down the tempo just a little. "We've got a lot of young guys who want to get it right to the net and get a shot," he said. That isn't always the best approach. "Sometimes you've got to slow it down a bit, set up a play and get a good shot; if not you waste the 30 seconds [shot clock] and give up the ball," he said.

Dealing with a shot clock was also a new experience for Keller in his first year in the league with the expansion Yorkton Bulldogs, but admits it keeps the game flowing. "It's not too bad. It's a lot quicker out there because you know you've got to make a play to make things happen," he said. It's a case of finding an open man with a pass, or working to get yourself open to take the shot.

In lacrosse the shot can come from anywhere: overhand, sidearm, bounced to the net, and even behind-the-back shots are taken. Keller said the fancier shots tend to surface when the team is in control of the game on the scoreboard. "When you're up a few you can try to be a little more fancy," he said, noting he has used the behind-the-back shot on a few occasions. "I think the fans like to see that kind of stuff."

For Keller, holding a lacrosse stick is almost second nature. "I've been playing lacrosse ever since Grade 5, I guess about 11 years, but it's always been field until now." Moving to box was not as big an adjustment as one might expect. "It wasn't too big an adjustment, just some different rules to get used too," he said.

Keller admitted lacrosse was not his first love of sporting life the way hockey was, noting the game has not been very high profile in Saskatchewan in the past. However, in 2002, being part of the Saskatchewan Junior Men's team, which captured the national field title in Kelowna, B.C., and the new box lacrosse league, had Keller more focused on the game than he ever had been before.

While he did tear up the lacrosse floor, Keller admitted his first love will remain hockey. "I never really took lacrosse too seriously until the last couple of years but hockey will always be number one," he said.

Over the Airwaves

When it comes to recognizable Saskatchewan names associated with hockey, one of most famous never played an organized game after completing college. The person himself suggests he is living proof hockey is not a matter of genetics, given that his father is a member of the Hockey Hall of Fame as a player. Still, few hockey fans in Saskatchewan, or across Canada for that matter, would not know who Dick Irvin is.

Nearly 40 years on Hockey Night in Canada broadcasts have made both Irvin's visage and smooth voice familiar to this country's hockey faithful. Irvin is modest about his recognition, saying it is far less him, and much more the show itself. "It's the show that's so ingrained in the Canadian mind or psyche. Hockey Night in Canada is very powerful. I found that out as I travelled...All of us on the show are just thrilled to be involved in it."

One night in particular where the popularity of the broadcasts came sharply into focus was when Irvin returned to Saskatchewan to do a segment of CBC's Hockey Day in Canada broadcast from Shaunavon in February 2004. "That time in Shaunavon was one of the most satisfying broadcast experiences I've ever had," he said. Irvin was one of only three HNIC staff in the Saskatchewan community, along with Ron McLean and Don Cherry, and he keenly remembers the reaction the community had to the surprise arrival of the Stanley Cup. "Even those of us on the show didn't know it was coming," said Irvin, who said the reaction at the Friday night banquet was great. "The next day they had the Cup on display at the arena. People were lined up all day just to see the Stanley Cup."

The nightly ritual of watching HNIC on CBC might well have evolved into a tradition in this country, but there is no doubt Irvin is part of the reason, having been involved in the broadcasts for just shy of four decades. The lockout during the 2004–05 season was all that stood between him and his 39th year on the show.

For Irvin to be on the show at all proved to be a matter of timing at a juncture of Irvin's life when he admits he was looking for something different. After two years of college at the University of Saskatchewan, Irvin completed his Commerce training at McGill University, a time when he also played hockey for both the Huskies and Redmen. He hung up his skates after his final game at McGill, never playing another organized game, and settled into a career as an accountant with Shell Canada.

However, after eight years of crunching numbers, he admits he was starting to look for a change, a feeling perhaps brought on by the death of his father, Dick Irvin Sr., in 1957. That appears to be where the fates of the game took control. It was 1961, and Canadian television was about to change with the launch of a new television network: CTV.

"I did a live interview with Brian McFarlane," said Irvin, recalling the interview started around Minor Hockey Week. "I had started coaching minor hockey in 1957. I had a Bantam team that won the Quebec provincial championship in 1961."

However, the interview also included a reminiscent look at his father's storied career, one that certainly set his son's interest squarely in the game of hockey. Dick Irvin Sr. was a fine player until a fractured skull ended his playing days, but his fame only grew as he moved behind the bench as a coach.

Irvin Sr. coached the Chicago Black Hawks to the Stanley Cup finals in 1931 but was fired because of a clash with owner Frederic McLaughlin at the beginning of the 1931–32 season. Then he took over the Toronto Maple Leafs, who had lost their first six games, and guided them to their first (as the Leafs) Stanley Cup championship. Irvin went to the Montreal Canadiens in 1940 and remained there through the 1954–55 season, winning three more Stanley Cups, in 1944, 1946 and 1953.

With such a career to recount, Irvin Jr. admitted his interview with McFarlane just flowed. In fact, he said with a chuckle, McFarlane "couldn't shut me up."

Obviously McFarlane liked what he heard, and how it was said, because within a few days he had offered the then 29-year-old accountant a job as his sports assistant at CTV. "I started May 8, 1961 for $75 a week. That's why they couldn't get anyone with experience. I spent the next 30 years there."

The job with CTV still allowed Irvin an opportunity to freelance with HNIC, initially part-time, and eventually evolving into a full-time thing beside his play-by-play partner Danny Gallivan. Working with Gallivan still tops Irvin's list of memories. "I spent 17 years beside Danny Gallivan. A lot of young announcers would give their right arm to do 17 games beside Danny Gallivan."

When it comes to memories of the game, Irvin doesn't have the mind set to pick out the best player he ever saw, or the best game he ever broadcast. "I don't have a game. I don't have a player.

It's just the whole experience." It's a case of simply seeing too many great players and great games to pick out particular ones. "I've seen All Star games since 1938," he said. In 1938, he was allowed out of school and rode the train to Toronto to watch the Leafs play a playoff game against Chicago. "I've seen a Stanley Cup playoff game in every decade since the 1930s."

However, one event he did take part in rates special mention by the veteran broadcaster. "I was the English MC the night they closed the Montreal Forum, March 11, 1996. That was a night I'll never forget."

Considering his father's long tenure as Canadiens coach, and the fact he himself moved from Regina, where he grew up, to Montreal when he was 19, the ties to the Forum were strong. In one of Irvin's books—he has written six on the game he loves—he said he tried to estimate how many times he had walked through the doors at the fabled building. Combining Canadiens games, junior contests, ice shows, Harlem Globetrotter exhibitions and numerous other events, "I figure around 5,000, but that's strictly a guess." Irvin's tie to the Forum includes doing radio broadcasts on Canadiens games for more than 20 years, a time he followed the team on the road as well to broadcast games back to Montreal. As an author he has written such hockey works as The Habs, Behind the Bench and In the Crease: Goaltenders Look at Life in the NHL.

On the night of the Forum's closure Irvin said the only members of the Montreal Canadiens on the ice were those already inducted into the Hockey Hall of Fame, among those only two were Westerners, Elmer Lach from Nokomis, Saskatchewan, and Ken Reardon from Winnipeg, who both played for Irvin's father. "All the players [at the ceremony] gathered in the dressing room which was just about where it had always been...and there was Elmer Lach and Ken Reardon just like the first time I was in the dressing room with my Dad 56 years earlier…Talk about seeing a life flash before your eyes. That sent a chill up my spine when I realized that."

It was a moment of déjà vu for Irvin, who grew up in Regina, spending his school year winters involved in the sport, but a long way from his father who was coaching in the NHL. "Once I started school, started Kindergarten, he didn't want me moving around during hockey season, so I stayed in Regina. He [dad] would live in a hotel in Toronto for the season."

Irvin does recall watching hockey as a youngster in the Queen City, following the Vics and the Aces. He remembers talk that one goaltender moved between the teams in a trade for a cow.

Also fondly recalled was an Allan Cup final between Regina and Sydney in 1941, a five-game series with the first team to six points taking the cup. Played in May, long after the NHL season was over, his father was home to watch the games. "I remember him cheering. It was the only time I remember him actually cheering at a hockey game." Sydney had won two and the third game was a tie, meaning Sydney needed only one more point to clinch the Cup, but Regina persevered to win, taking the final game on what Irvin termed a "dark, stormy night at the old Queen City Stadium." Irvin said the Regina team was a strong one, with future NHLers such as Grant Warwick, who won the Calder trophy in 1942, "Sugar" Jim Henry and Garth Boesch.

As for following his father's career, Irvin said it was radio broadcasts, and those too were rare since games originated in Toronto, and his father spent years in Montreal. "I lived my life, as far as dad's teams were concerned, from a distance."

On those rare occasions the Canadiens played the Leafs, it was great; otherwise Irvin said he was most often more interested in the out-of-town scores than the game itself on the radio.

But even at that young age Irvin said there was something of a precursor of what was to come. "The next morning after a game [on radio] I'd go out on our backyard rink on Angus Street and I'd broadcast the games like Foster Hewitt. I'd be skating around yelling out the play," he said, adding with a laugh one "crabby" neighbour even complained about the noise he made.

From his youth in Regina following the exploits of his father's teams from afar, to his near-four decades in broadcasting hockey to a nation, Irvin has seen the game evolve. Today, he says fans are seeing the best players overall to ever play the game. "I think that players are better. Players are more talented generally [in] shooting and skating." Irvin credits the European invasion for that. "We are now seeing the best players in the world everyday."

However, the game is still watered down, dragged down by there simply being too many teams. In the past great players such as Maurice "Rocket" Richard or Bobby Hull, were surrounded by a team deep in talent, with often several players destined for the Hockey Hall of Fame. "Now most teams have a star or two, but that's it," said Irvin, adding he recalled watching Paul Kariya stand out one night with the Anaheim Mighty Ducks, "but he was the only strong player on the team."

Attrition is what Irvin sees as the key to returning quality to the game at the NHL level. "If we had 22, maybe 24 teams, then we'd see the best hockey we've ever seen."

It's an insight to the game's future provided by someone who has seen much of the game from the broadcast booth. Irvin has covered more than 2,500 NHL games on television and radio—leaving little wonder why he is a sought-after speaker, an activity that has taken him from Newfoundland to British Columbia. In 1988 he won the Foster Hewitt Award for excellence in hockey broadcasting and was inducted into the media section of the Hockey Hall of Fame, joining his father in the shrine to the game both loved so much.

Clare Drake and the Bears

When it comes to coaching at the university level, few have put together the career Clare Drake did as coach of the University of Alberta Golden Bears. Drake coached the Bears for 28 years, amassing 697 victories, a record among North American coaches at the time of his retirement in 1989, although it has since been eclipsed.

For Drake, the opportunity to coach started in Yorkton, Saskatchewan. When asked if he played as a youth, he was quick with the retort, "[Didn't] everybody? It sure seemed that way."

Drake came from "a pretty good sporting background," starting with his father Clarence J. Drake who taught at Burke School in the city for 40 years. As a youngster he tried all the sports, but said one of the best memories was of future National Hockey League player Metro Prystai, who would go on to score a Stanley Cup winning goal in his career. "I was his winger in Grade 8," he said with a chuckle.

Drake believes his Yorkton roots were an important start

for him. "The idea of coming out of Yorkton was so great for anybody who liked sports. There was great opportunity to try sports there."

On the ice Drake was accomplished enough as a player to play a year of junior, before heading to the University of British Columbia where he played for three years, becoming team captain. "We ended up being a pretty strong team," he said, noting the team was inducted into the UBC Sports Hall of Fame.

While his playing days would include a year as a player-coach in Dusseldorf, Germany after college, he soon found himself in Edmonton as a teacher. He taught for three years in Edmonton at Strathcona Composite High School before joining the staff of the Faculty of Physical Education at the U of A, and taking up his duties as coach of the hockey Golden Bears for a near 30-year run.

Drake said he never dreamed of a three-decade tenure at the helm of the Golden Bears. "You really don't think that far ahead, but it was where I wanted to be in terms of coaching at the university level. You get really highly motivated athletes. The university has a good reputation, and the sport environment has a good reputation."

Hockey players at Canadian colleges are there for a true love of the game, not motivated by the push of parents, or the lure of big money contracts, but rather by an inner pride in the game. "The players are focused on two things. They're focused on an education, and they really want to get better as hockey players," said Drake.

Of course the college game changed through the years Drake stood behind the U of A bench, with the quality of hockey improving. "There's been definite improvement. We always had really good players on an individual level, but now there's a better depth in terms of talent across the country."

In general terms hockey players are bigger and faster today, and that is reflected in the college game too, and has been aided by better coaching. "The coaching has really improved over the years. When I started most teams only had one coach and that limits in terms of what you can do."

It helps the college game in Canada too that they now attract older players. "There's a lot of kids thinking about going into college hockey that didn't used to consider Canadian colleges," said Drake. Now players who have gone through the major junior ranks, losing their American college eligibility, turn to the Canadian system after their junior days are done. That means college freshmen are often 21 years of age, making the Canadian game very high calibre.

That's a contrast to when Drake coached. In 1989, when he retired, he said teams might have had two, three, four graduates of Western Hockey League programs. Today it's not unusual to have 15. "The calibre of university hockey [today] is just below the AHL," said Drake. "It's a cut above the best junior, not much, but a little, just because guys are older. It's a very good calibre of play."

That isn't to say Drake didn't coach some great hockey teams. In fact, he won six national hockey championships with the Golden Bears, but the teams were younger. He pointed to a string of three championships in a row, 1978–80. Two key players, Don Spring and Randy Gregg, joined the team at 17 and 18 respectively. While obviously strong players, both went on to the NHL, with Gregg capturing five Stanley Cups with the Edmonton Oilers. They joined the college ranks much younger than is the norm today. "They kind of grew up in the program back then," said Drake.

While Drake is best known for his job behind the hockey bench, he also pulled off a unique double as a coach, coaching the Golden Bears football team to a national championship in 1967, and the following spring repeating the national prize with the hockey edition of the Golden Bears. "That was quite a thrill," he said with modesty, adding both championship finals were nail biters.

The football Bears' Vanier Cup victory in Toronto was not a huge surprise given the team had some excellent prospects, such as Ed Molstad and John Wilson, both 230-pound seniors who signed professional contracts with the Edmonton Eskimos the following spring. The team also had a strong group of assistant coaches, such as line coach Roy Stevenson and backfield coach Jim Donlevy, who had been with the team for several seasons. The Bears had also beaten the McMaster University Marauders, who were to be the eastern representatives in the Vanier Cup game, by a score of 11–1 in a pre-season exhibition game.

"We were leading the game (the final) 10–9, but they were pushing us, and we were just kind of hanging on," recalled Drake, of a game played in the rain. McMaster had tried and failed to take the lead due to the wet field on one field goal, and had driven to the Bears' 17-yard line again. They chose to try to get in closer, and instead threw up an interception which sealed the two-point U of A crown.

Drake said it was an interesting time as he coached the gridiron Bears for four seasons. "When I was with the football team, I was also doing hockey by myself. The football team would practice from 5:15 to 6:30, and then I'd slip into the change room, take off my football cleats and put on my skates and go back out on the ice."

In the hockey final the situation was no less close. The Bears faced Loyola at the Montreal Forum in front of some 12,000 fans, one of the largest crowds to ever witness a Canadian college hockey final. At the end of the second the Bears trailed 4–2, but fought back in the third to tie it, and finally win it with a goal with only 17 seconds left on the clock. Ron Cebryk, who had scored three goals the night before against St. Francis Xavier, tied the game at 4–4, and also netted the winner.

"Thirty Alberta fans were happy, and 11,970 Quebec fans weren't," said Drake.

With six national championships to his coaching credit, Drake obviously saw a lot of great players wearing Golden Bear uniforms. However, when it comes to talking about the best, something he said he is always reluctant to do, he turned to a player from his old hometown of Yorkton. "Vern Pachal was one of the best players to ever play at the University of Alberta. He was definitely in the top three or four and maybe the top."

Pachal led the Bears in scoring in each of his three seasons, averaging about four points a game, the kind of stats Drake said, had the National Hockey League been larger than a six-team league at the time, would have meant Pachal playing there. "The NHL was only six teams and he was just below that at the time. If there had been 30 teams like there is now, he would have played in the NHL for a long time."

In addition to his years with the Bears, Drake took to the bench in a number of other situations as well. He stepped away from the U of A bench for a year to coach the Canadian Olympic team in 1980, along with Tom Watt and Lorne Davis. "That was the year of Herb Brooks' American miracle team [which won gold at the Lake Placid Games]. We had played them eight times over the year and beat them five times, and tied them once," he said. But at the games, a Canadian weakness in goal, a soft spot Drake said the team had all year, haunted the Canucks. "We just finished out of the medals. It was a 115-foot shot on goal that went in, and put us out of the medal round. I don't like to think about it."

In 1985, Drake was also head coach of Canada's first team at the Spengler Cup in Davos, Switzerland, with a team made up of half collegiate players, and half Canadians playing pro in

Europe. "It was a great place to play. The fans are unbelievable in Davos." Drake's grandson Michael Gavinet is now a pro in Europe himself, playing his rookie season in 2004–05 in the Finnish Elite League.

Following his retirement from the Bears, Drake turned to the NHL for a final stint at coaching, a situation he saw as a natural way to conclude a career. He spent time as an assistant coach under Bob Murdoch in Winnipeg with the now-moved Jets for two seasons, then worked with the San Jose Sharks and Dallas Stars with developmental programs.

When you look at Drake's career, it's not a surprise he has been honoured multiple times since retiring from the bench, including induction into the Alberta and Canadian Sport Hall of Fames, and a co-induction with his father into his hometown Yorkton's Sport Hall of Fame and Museum. The nomination to the Canadian Sports Hall of Fame is a definite highlight for Drake, who called it "a wonderful recognition." The U of A arena was also renamed Drake Arena in his honour.

Although the accolades have come, and the career is officially over, Drake remains interested in hockey, helping out with clinics with coaches from the Edmonton Oilers, and of course keeping an eye on the U of A and his beloved Golden Bears.

"I go over occasionally," he said of the university today. "We're hosting the National Championship in hockey the next two years [2005 and 2006], and I'm the honourary chairperson of that committee, so I'm doing some work with that.

"And, I'm doing some coaching clinics, which I really enjoy."

The Lightning and the Thunder

You might say Travis Clayton provides the lightning for the Wichita Thunder hockey club. Clayton, a native of Paradise Hill, Saskatchewan, is in his eighth season with the Central Hockey League franchise, and is carving his name into the team's record books, while at the same time steadily moving up the list in most of the league's offensive categories as well.

The current edition of the CHL is a fairly recent creation formed for the 1992–93 season, with teams in Wichita, Oklahoma City, Tulsa, Memphis, Fort Worth and Dallas, but that doesn't lessen the impact Clayton has had.

On a line with Alberta-born Jason Duda almost since day one in Wichita, the pair jostle for top spot in almost every team scoring category. "We've been together since my first year down here. It's just natural out there now. We know where each other will be," he said. He's not sure why the duo has clicked as well as it has. "He's good with the puck and has good patience, and I just read off him. We've got something that's pretty special."

The pair has also become good friends off the ice too, and that's a factor in the success of it. "That has a lot to do with it, when you're friends away from the rink you just get closer," said Clayton.

The pair does seem linked. For example, on November 27, 2002, Duda picked up four points versus Tulsa, becoming the first Thunder player to ever record 400 career points. Two nights later Clayton recorded four points of his own versus Corpus Christi, joining Jason Duda in the Thunder 400-point club. Who holds the team career marks in the end will likely be whoever plays the longest with the Thunder. For Clayton, that could mean the records will grow substantially, since he has no plans to retire anytime soon. "Hopefully I'll play for a while yet," said the 28-year-old (in 2005). "I just love the game. I'd like to play six, seven more years at least."

Regardless of how long Clayton pushes his Wichita career, his numbers are already impressive. In games played he has 489, which is 11 better than Duda, and 178 more than Sean O'Reilly who sits third on the list. He has 240 goals, only five better than Duda, but 97 more than Bob Berg who sits third in career goals. Clayton also tops the team list in power play goals, short-handed goals, shoot-out goals, and game-winning goals, just ahead of Duda in every instance. Clayton's 365 assists is also a team career best, 11 better than Duda, and a whopping 178 assists better than Bob Berg in third. His 604 points is also a team best. The numbers are such that Clayton is already in the top-10 in career goals, assists and points in the CHL as well.

Scoring is what Clayton said he knows he must do to play at the CHL level. "Smaller guys like me have to put up the points. I'm not there to fight or check," he said. At the same time career statistics are not something Clayton, or linemate Duda, worry about. "We don't really talk about it. We just take it a year at a time…I've never really thought about career records. I just go out and play the game."

For a small, gifted scorer, just playing can be a grind since he inevitably faces the opposition's best defensive players. "I just go out and play. I try not to worry about it, but it gets frustrating some nights."

As for his start in the game, Clayton said he can't remember the first time he put on a pair of skates. "I know my dad had a lot to do with it, with getting me skating at the rink, and out on the pond."

Clayton's earliest organized hockey was in Paradise Hill, a community that, while small, had a fairly new arena for the local kids to learn the game. In time, he advanced to a team from the area, which would have him playing on the same team as future National Hockey League player Wade Redden. The two Saskatchewan boys remain good friends. "It's always nice to see someone that you know going to the NHL. That's just great."

At 16, Clayton made his first move to play hockey, heading about 75 minutes down the road to play for the North Battleford North Stars of the Saskatchewan Junior Hockey League. He said not having to move until he was 16 was probably a positive for his development. "I think it was. I was from a small town but we still played Double "A" Bantam which was the top in Saskatchewan. We were playing some pretty good hockey."

Moving to an SJHL team close to home helped too, keeping him in contact with family through his years with the Stars. "Mom and dad and most of my aunts and uncles drove down to home games. I don't think mom and dad missed a home game my whole time there," he said.

While with the Stars, Clayton came under the influence of two coaches, Todd McLellan and Blaine Gusdal, who both helped mold him as a player. "I learned so much from those two guys, just the little things about hockey, like how to play the defensive game," he said. "And, how to take care of yourself off the ice."

Clayton would toil nearly five seasons in a Stars uniform, coming close to a championship which has so far eluded him throughout his career. "When I was 18, 19, 20 we were in the finals two of three years, and the third year we lost in the North [semi] final," he said. "It was kind of disappointing not to win. Definitely we were right there.

"But, Weyburn knocked us out both years in the final. They had been there before, so we had to knock off a champion, and we came up short." Today, the search for a championship with the Thunder stays a motivation, since a crown has always eluded him so far.

Although Clayton would have an outstanding career in the Battlefords (his 235 career assists remain a team record), in retrospect he admits he would have moved on with his career a season or two sooner than he did. Playing in the SJHL, Clayton had hoped to secure an American college scholarship, but in his final season as a 20-year-old, no full-ride offers came his way. The University of Maine did make a partial offer, but it would have cost Clayton an additional $30,000, so college was not to be.

That was surprising for the talented forward, considering at 18, he was getting lots of college scouts talking to him, including those from Northern Michigan, Ohio and Lake Superior, all noted as having strong hockey programs. "I wish I had taken a full ride when I was 18," he said. "I'm not disappointed with the choices I made, I'm happy with what I'm doing, but I definitely think I would have taken an early scholarship if I could do it again. I have talked to lots of guys that went to school, and they said it was great.

"I thought they [offers] would always be there when the time came, but it wasn't that way."

With the college experience no longer in the cards for Clayton, he began to set his sights on playing in Europe, but he never got to buy the airplane tickets. Instead, then-Wichita coach Brian Wells invited him to the Thunder camp. "He [Wells] did a lot of recruiting from the SJ," said Clayton.

Once in Wichita, Clayton liked not only the team and league, but the city too. "It's a pretty good little city. They really support their hockey team through the good times and the bad."

Clayton said interest in hockey still lags behind college basketball and football in Wichita, but they draw about 4,000 fans a game just the same. The hockey is also better than most realize. "It's definitely improved over the last few years. There's a lot of talent in this league now," said Clayton. "It's pretty high calibre actually."

As high calibre as the CHL may be, Clayton has proven to be among the league's elite since his arrival in Wichita, and his efforts have garnered recognition. He was voted the Thunder Selfless Player of the Year in both 1998–99 and 1999–00, leading the Thunder in scoring each season, winning the award again in 2002. And, in his most recent campaign, he was a Special President's Selection to the CHL All Star Game, where he picked up two goals and an assist.

In spite of racking up impressive numbers every season in Wichita, Clayton has only had a cup of coffee stint in a higher league, playing only a dozen American Hockey League contests. He says his size is probably what keeps that door closed.

"I'm only 5-foot-8, and nowadays 6-foot you might still be too small," he said. "I think that has a lot to do with it...I can't complain about things, you wish you could have gone to a higher level, but things have really worked out for me here too." That's fine, since Clayton is comfortable in Wichita. "They've treated me great right through the organization, and the city. It's pretty much home for me now."

While Clayton said he still occasionally talks of going to Europe to play, he is becoming content to look at Wichita as the starting and ending place of his professional career. "Right now I'm just happy playing hockey here," he said, adding it's a great way to make a living. "It's definitely not like the big boys [in the NHL], but we're definitely making a living.

"I know guys back home [in Saskatchewan] making real good money in the oil fields and they'd love to be playing hockey."

Happy to Be a Pioneer

Murray Armstrong might not be a household name for most Saskatchewan hockey fans, but if you were a fan of the University of Denver (DU) Pioneers you would recognize the name. Armstrong, who grew up in Semans, Saskatchewan, was coach of the Pioneers for 21 seasons, including capturing five national championships. Armstrong joined the DU Pioneers as coach in 1957, and a year later, in 1958, he led the team to the NCAA crown by defeating North Dakota 6-2.

In 1960 the Pioneers were back on top, claiming their second NCAA crown, defeating Michigan Tech 5–3, and again in 1961 defeating St. Lawrence 12–2. The 1960–61 team developed by Armstrong has been called one of the greatest college hockey teams ever. The team won 30, lost but one and tied one, taking the WCHA and NCAA titles in the process. In 1960–61 Armstrong received the Spencer Penrose Award, NCAA Division I Coach of the Year and WCHA Coach of the Year honours.

In 1968, Armstrong and the Pioneers were back, defeating

North Dakota 4–0 to capture their fourth NCAA title, with Armstrong named WCHA Coach of the Year. A year later in 1969, the Pioneers defeated Cornell 4–3 to win its fifth NCAA title. "I was there for 21 years," said Armstrong, 89. "The NCAA used to have the "Big Four" teams for the nationals. My team went to 11 National Championships, and we won five times. We should have won it twice more." In one final Armstrong said they had a sure goal disallowed that cost them the title. In the other he takes the full blame. "In the other one I didn't give them the pep talk I should have."

Armstrong said he felt he could do well in DU from the outset. "When I went there I told the Athletic Director 'I'll give you a national championship in three years or I'll resign'. I got the National Championship in the second year."

With 21 years at the Pioneer helm, Armstrong said he saw the American college game change. "There are a lot more teams and good athletes involved now," he said. "It wasn't as good when I coached as it is now, but it wasn't bad hockey either."

The championships show success, although Armstrong said he measured his career differently. "I don't think of it based on the wins or on the losses. I think of the successes of the boys I coached," he said. "I am so proud of the successes of these boys on their lives and businesses and families…I still see and hear from a lot of them, and all of them have become very successful. They have happy lives too."

Often he saw the greatest joys in the Canadian boys he recruited to the program. "They were often boys that didn't have a thing," he said, adding their families were so happy to have their boys offered a full scholarship that promised an education along with hockey. He said often he was asked if the family had to sign a deal and his reply was "I'll give you a hearty handshake."

"I always told them if somebody offered something better

for them to take it…Not one boy said he was going to come and didn't, and not once did I refuse them once they said yes."

With such attachment to players, picking out the best he ever coached is not something Armstrong relished doing, but he did say Saskatchewan-born defenceman Keith Magnuson and Manitoba's Bill Masterton were two great players to pass through the Pioneer program.

In selecting players, Armstrong said he liked to talk to people about prospects. If those he spoke with said they were great players, great students, they had his interest. However if anyone added the word "but" to a discussion "I lost interest," he said. "I wanted good people. If I couldn't get good people, I didn't want them no matter how they played hockey. Not once did I have to go to the police with one of my players in 21 seasons."

If there was a key to Armstrong's success, it was drawing on his own experiences through the years of playing. "I learned to be honest with the boys, and to be fair, and to live a good life," he said. "I think I set a good example when I was in Denver. I never drank. I never smoked. I never fooled around on my wife, and we've been married 62 years. When I was playing there were guys with a girlfriend in every city we went to. I lost respect for them."

Armstrong's coaching career was built on a foundation as a player which started back in a small town Saskatchewan rink. "I grew up in Semans. My father was the blacksmith there. They had a closed-in rink. From as early as I can remember, until I was 12 and we moved to Regina, I played there," he said, adding the move to the capital city expanded his hockey. "That's where I started playing organized hockey."

Armstrong said playing hockey was simply the natural thing for him to do. "It was the only thing I knew. I knew hockey, and I knew baseball in the summer."

By the age of 16 Armstrong was playing for the Regina Pats

under Al Ritchie, and it wasn't long before he was off to New York to play with the amateur Rovers. "So I guess I was a pretty good junior player," he said. The Rovers, while amateur, were a good team and included Craig and Murray Patrick on the team.

"I was drafted out of that league by the Toronto Maple Leafs," said Armstrong. "But I didn't play very much in Toronto [only three games]." Instead he played three seasons with the Leaf affiliate Syracuse Stars. In the 1938–39 season, he recorded 27 goals and 54 points in only 50 games, but come playoff time for Toronto, he was not called up.

Armstrong said he went to see Commie Smyth at the end of the season. "I told them I was disappointed I didn't get called up to the playoffs, and that in missing that chance I missed the extra money from the playoffs too," he said. "Mr. Smyth called in his secretary and told her to have a cheque made out to 'Mr. Armstrong for $300'."

Even with a cheque to make up for the playoff bonuses Armstrong felt he had lost, he still asked for a trade to open doors to the NHL. The Leafs obliged, sending Armstrong, Charlie Conacher, Busher Jackson and Buzz Boll to the New York Americans.

With the Americans, in the then seven-team NHL, Armstrong tied for eighth in league scoring in the 1939–40 season with 36 points. That same year his salary was $3,000. "But they raised it to $4,500 after that year."

The next season though, Armstrong would have back pain. He would play most games, but his performance dropped off. Back in Regina after the season, his doctor said it was either early signs of spinal meningitis, syphilis or a slipped disc. "I was scared to death," he said, but tests confirmed it was only a disc problem. He was sent to the Mayo Clinic in Minneapolis for an operation. "After they did the operation I never had a pain in my back again," he said. He took the train, stayed over in Winnipeg one night to make connections, then spent 10 days in hospital, took the train back, and the bill came to $619.37, said Armstrong.

Armstrong presented the bill to Red Dutton with the Americans, but never was reimbursed. "To this day they still owe me $619.37," he said with a chuckle.

The Americans would eventually fold, and Armstrong would turn away from hockey in 1942 as the world was gripped in the second great war. "I joined the Canadian Army. I played with, and coached the army team in Regina," he said. "We won the Saskatchewan championship. We had to play Flin Flon. We met them in Saskatoon."

It was in that game that Armstrong learned a lesson that would stick through his years of coaching. The game was in the third period and Flin Flon was leading 5–1. Armstrong went to take a face-off and the Flin Flon player began beaking about how he thought the Regina team was supposed to be so good because of the professionals on the roster such as Armstrong, Byron "Butch" McDonald, Don Metz and William "Red" Tilson.

Armstrong went to the bench and passed on the remarks made by his opponent. "There were 11 minutes to go, and when it ended we had won 6–5," he said. "I've used that a lot since then. When you're beating someone sympathize with them. Don't be a smart ass, or those things can happen to you."

With his back operation on his file, Armstrong could not serve overseas, and was eventually granted an early discharge, and immediately joined the Detroit Red Wings in mid-season. He spent two more seasons before being released. "They took on a young fellow by the name of Gordie Howe instead," said Armstrong with a chuckle.

While that was the end of his NHL career, he keeps some great memories. "One thing that I always remember was the last game I played. It was for the Stanley Cup championship in Boston. Boston beat us 2–1, and I got the only goal. It was the last goal I scored in the National League."

Armstrong would play two more years in the minors then return to Regina and become the Pats coach for eight seasons. At the time the Pats were financed by Montreal, and the Canadiens took most of the talent to play in the east. "We had mostly second grade players," said Armstrong. "But in eight years we went to the National Championships four times, but we never won it."

With the success of the Pats, Denver University came calling. "Some of the boys that played for me in Regina went there for a couple of years. I think they put in a good word for me, and then they [the university] called me," he said. The rest is history as they say, and Armstrong's career is one which has garnered him recognition from several sources since his retirement. In 1974, Armstrong was inducted into the Colorado Sports Hall of Fame, received the 1976 Denver U.S.A. Citizen by Choice Award and the Lester Patrick Trophy in New York in 1977, and was inducted into the Saskatchewan Sports Hall of Fame.

Armstrong said he was just happy to be a Pioneer. While he had interest in coaching in the pros, he was at home at DU. "I couldn't have asked for a better life," he said, adding he turned down an offer from Muzz Patrick with the New York Rangers. "I was happy in Denver. I enjoyed coaching the young boys."

A Lifelong Learning Curve

As a hockey player, every situation you find yourself in during a career is a learning experience, one you can take something away from which can help you in situations down the road. At least that is the philosophy Dirk Graham came to follow as he made his way from an outdoor rink in Regina to a career in the National Hockey League which saw him play 772 regular season games over 13 years. For Graham it was a case of having to learn lessons, often the hard way, as he progressed up the ladder toward his ultimate goal of playing in the NHL.

The first steps onto the ice went smoothly enough. It was a short walk across the street from his home in Regina to skate as often as he wanted. "Like every other kid in Saskatchewan and all across Canada I just started skating at a young age. We had a rink across the street in the Taylor Field parking lot," he said. "When I was four or five years old I was out there."

Hockey quickly became a passion for Graham too. "Absolutely. In Canada hockey is like baseball down here [in the

United States], it's what every little kid dreams of doing. You always remember watching Hockey Night in Canada on Saturday night. You grew up idolizing the guys you saw on TV…It is pretty much an ingrained thing. If we weren't skating or playing on the ice, we were playing shinny on the street."

For Graham, his boyhood heroes wore the black and yellow of the Boston Bruins. "In my era I was a big fan of the Boston Bruins, so obviously Bobby Orr was a favourite. He was just coming into his own, and really changing the game defensively."

Derek Sanderson was another Bruin whom Graham watched closely. "The way he played, he was kind of similar to my style," he said. In Graham's case though, it was a style that would evolve out of necessity through his career.

After moving up through the minor system in Regina, Graham would play junior with the Regina Pats. "I was very fortunate in that respect. At that time there wasn't as much moving around to play as there is now. There were 10–15 guys on the Pats right from Regina."

While Graham might have been able to enjoy home cooking as a Pat, on the ice things weren't all that enjoyable. "We struggled pretty good. We had some pretty lean years…But, you learn from all different experiences, whether winning or losing. It just depends what you take out of it."

Playing with the Pats was, in the end, a bittersweet experience for Graham. "You end up playing for the top team in the city, so it's pretty gratifying, but at the same time you're losing a lot of games, so it was pretty frustrating."

On the personal side though, Graham developed well as a Pat, reaching the 100-point plateau in his last two seasons of junior. While impressive stats, he would soon have to learn offence was not to be his bread and butter as a pro. Drafted 89th overall in 1979 by Vancouver, Graham was assigned to the Canucks farm team in Dallas, and was suddenly expected to play a style that was no longer offensive. "In junior hockey that happens a lot once you turn pro, you have to change your game because the level of talent goes up so much. There's a lot of very talented players and you have to adjust your game, and it takes a while to do that."

In Graham's case the adjustment was not as smooth as he may have liked, and he was moved down to the Toledo Goaldiggers of the International Hockey League. "It was the old IHL. It was a pretty rough and tough league," said Graham. Initially the move was a hard one to take. "But I ended up having a very good experience down there."

It was a case of accepting change and realizing that change presents a challenge you must respond to. In Graham's situation that meant accepting he had to grow as a player. "You kind of have to come to the realization on your own to realize what you have to do to make it to the next level. You have to be willing to adjust. You have to learn."

For Graham that meant moving away from thoughts of 100-point seasons to concentrate on the other side of the game—defence. "You have to learn the defensive game, and adjust to it." Graham said even the best offensive players in the pros recognize they have to play defence too, something scorers in junior are often not expected to contribute. "In junior if you're putting up the numbers they really don't expect you to play defence that much," he said.

Graham said it was still tough accepting the assignment to Toledo. "It just seemed I was so far away from the dream of making the NHL," he said.

That's where Toledo coach Bill Inglis stepped in and helped Graham refocus his efforts. "He was very key in me getting that second chance," said Graham. "…At that point in my career he really focused me on the goals I wanted to accomplish. At the time

I was starting to wonder, is this really worth it? Is anything going to happen for me in hockey?"

Once he got past the feelings associated with being sent down, Graham said he started to enjoy his time in Toledo, and now looks on it as one of his best hockey memories. "It was a couple of my best years playing hockey. We had a lot of fun. We had a very close team. It ended up being an experience that was very rewarding."

At the same time it helped that the Goaldiggers won two league championships in 1982 and '83, helping keep NHL eyes looking at the talent on the Toledo roster. It was during a league final Graham was watched by Glen Sonmor, another "Saskatchewanite" from Moose Jaw, searching out talent for the Minnesota North Stars, who ultimately gave Graham a new deal and a chance at the NHL. "Once you get the opportunity, it's what you do with it."

Graham made the best of it, breaking in with the Stars for his first NHL game during the 1983–84 season. He would play parts of five seasons in Minnesota. "We had some very skilled players," he said, pointing to the likes of Dino Ciccarelli and Neal Broten. "But we could never get over the hump."

Looking back Graham said the Stars had the talent to succeed, but the team was never close enough as a group to take it to the final level. "I think that's what really makes sports in general, and hockey unique, you can't succeed unless you have that closeness, and camaraderie," he said.

In retirement Graham appreciates the feeling of belonging to a team even more. "You don't miss the game, you miss the camaraderie. You miss accomplishing goals as a team of 20 guys," he said.

The fact that the Stars couldn't get it done made ascending to the NHL another sort of bittersweet occurrence. "There was a little bit of gratification that you finally made it to the NHL, but once you're there the ultimate goal changes to winning the Stanley Cup."

The Cup eluded Graham in Minnesota, and then suddenly he was dealt to Chicago part-way through the 1987–88 season. The move was a surprise, especially since the Stars and Blackhawks had developed quite a rivalry in that era. "There were a lot of scraps, and I was involved in a few of them," said Graham. Again, a move that at first took a period of adjustment to accept turned out to be the right move for Graham. "As I look back on it now it was a blessing in disguise," he said.

As a Blackhawk, Graham had both his greatest personal and team success in the NHL. The team would win the President's Trophy in 1992, and would go to the Stanley Cup finals the same year. Not winning that Cup remains the biggest regret of his career. "It was very, very disappointing. We worked so hard that year. We accomplished so much," he said, "...But then you have to step back and look at the kind of team that beat us." The team was the Pittsburgh Penguins led by the likes of Mario Lemieux and Jaromir Jagr. "It was an unbelievable hockey team that we lost to.

"It was a learning experience too, just what it took to get to that level, to play in a final."

On a personal level too, Graham emerged as a Blackhawk. He would wear the Captain's "C" for six seasons. "That was a very rewarding experience to wear the "C", especially for an original six team," he said.

Graham was also honored with the Frank J. Selke Trophy as the NHL's best defensive forward for the 1990–91 season. He posted NHL career highs in goals (33), assists (45) and points (78) in 1988–89. And his 10 shorthanded goals that season set a Blackhawks' franchise record and equaled the fourth most to have been recorded in a single NHL season.

As a Hawk, Graham also came under the guidance of coach Mike Keenan, a coach many players loved to hate, although for Graham the tough Keenan was a good fit. "Everybody has their opinion about Mike. Mike Keenan did a great deal for me in my career. He pushed me to levels I didn't think I was capable of achieving…He challenged me to reach for new levels.

"Sometimes when you make the NHL you think that's enough, but he pushed me to be Captain, and to help lead a team to the [Stanley Cup] finals.

"He pushed me to reach for more and not be satisfied with what I'd accomplished up to that point."

After his playing days came to an end in 1995, Graham stepped in as an assistant coach with Chicago, and then 59 games as head coach, before moving on to scouting for a few years. Now he's back on the bench, assuming the head spot with the Springfield Falcons of the American Hockey League. He said in molding himself as a coach, he tries to bring the best of what others gave to him through the years. "I think every coach takes a little bit of everybody they've come in contact with," he said. "You take little pieces of what fits with your personality, and fits into your style.

"But, you have to be honest and up front with players, and respect the players. If you try to be something you're not, players will recognize that and they won't respond."

Back on the bench, Graham said he has no aspirations to return to the NHL as a coach. He said when he first became a coach he realized what he enjoyed most was helping players achieve their goals. "I really felt it put me in a position to help players accomplish their dreams. Young players have dreams and when you can help them achieve those dreams, it's a pretty special feeling."

Graham sees the opportunity in the minors to influence young players that he wouldn't have in the NHL. "I enjoy this level much more. If I can help kids to the next level, that's great."

Close Calls

The Calgary Flames' run at the Stanley Cup in the spring of 2004 caught the imagination of the country, as they made it to the finals before bowing out to Tampa Bay.

Rhett Warrener, who was born in Shaunavon and grew up in Saskatoon, patrolled the Flames blueline throughout the run. He said the experience was one of the most memorable in his career. "The situation in Calgary was so special for everyone...It was a different feeling because it was a Canadian team in the final, and everyone wanted to see the Cup back in Canada."

The feeling of the Flames came from the top down in some regards, starting with head coach Darryl Sutter. "It was probably the best group of coaches I've played under," said Warrener. "They got everything out of everybody they could. He's as intense as you can imagine, but he's a great person, and wants the best for his players."

Warrener said the overtime loss in Game 6 of the finals, on a goal by Martin St. Louis in front of the Flames faithful, will stick with him forever. Calgary could have capped their Cinderella season that game, but it slipped away. "We had a chance to take it all here at home. It looked like it was our time, that the stars were aligned, but I guess not.

"It's the things like that that stick with you... We had our chance, and let it get away."

Even in the loss Warrener said he recognizes the Flames were a special team through the spring of 2004. "We had a great group of guys. Everybody was on the same page, and believed the same things, and wanted the same thing."

For the Flames, they sort of evolved into a contender, and Warrener said there wasn't exactly one moment in the season they knew they were destined for the finals. "We had goals on our team. The first step of that was making the playoffs."

Once in the playoffs things jelled, and the team's confidence grew. "We all believed it didn't matter who we played, if we played our game, we could win," said Warrener.

In many ways Warrener was a leader on the Flames based on experience alone. Twice before he was part of teams making it to the final dance—first with Florida and then with Buffalo. With the Panthers, Warrener said he was so young he just sort of basked in the experience. With Buffalo, Warrener would also go to the finals, an experience different from Florida where everybody was just excited to be there. In Buffalo they wanted a winner.

"The people in Buffalo are great. Playing hockey there is about as close to a Canadian hockey town as you're going to get in the States," he said.

It's a case where each experience has its memories. "They are all fairly special, but the last one [with Calgary] was something, especially with them missing the playoffs for seven years."

There was also an atmosphere on the team that elevated the Calgary experience. "I felt this one was one we could have won," he said. In Florida it was so unexpected to even make the finals. "And Buffalo was more businesslike, there was more of an expectation to it."

Warrener said it's a case where any time a team takes a run at the coveted Stanley Cup, it's likely to be something special. "I think every time a team gets the right group of guys with the right motivation you have something unique," he said.

Warrener has also come to recognize that when it comes to making a Stanley Cup run, goaltending is the key. With Calgary it was Miikka Kiprusoff. In Florida it was John Vanbiesbrouck, and in Buffalo it was Dominik Hasek. "You can't win at this level without goaltending," he said, adding he's been fortunate to patrol in front of some of the game's hottest netminders through playoff runs.

Like most NHLers-to-be, Warrener began skating in Shaunavon at an age almost too young to recall. "I can remember skating pushing the chair around the rink."

Warrener said it was a definite positive growing up in a small town because he got to play lots of hockey. "I was playing on two teams. I only had one day off a week. It was just more ice time than you could dream of in a big city like Saskatoon."

Warrener's family would move to Saskatoon and his hockey career would start to take greater focus. He would move through the minor system and end up with the Saskatoon Blades of the Western Hockey League, the same team his older brother Trevor had played for. "I was pretty lucky to stay at home and be well-fed and play in front of family and friends," he said, adding it wasn't exactly the path his older brother had suggested. "He actually tried to talk me into playing with the Saskatoon Titans," he said.

Going to the Titans, Warrener would have remained eligible for an American college scholarship. "But education was never really a big thing for me," he said, so he choose the major junior path.

Warrener said his time with the Blazers was good, especially with the team playing so well in the early 1990s. "We had really good teams when I played for the Blades. We really had everyone chipping in... We had lots of guys that didn't make it to the pro level, but at the junior level we were very, very good."

However, the ultimate prize of a Memorial Cup never came to Warrener. "We were always right there, expecting to win. We lost in Game 7 to Kamloops to go to the Memorial Cup."

Still, Warrener impressed enough through Junior to be selected 27th overall in the 1994 draft by the Florida Panthers. "I was drafted by Florida and it was a perfect fit because they were an expansion team, and were looking to add some young guys," he said. Although the Panthers were an expansion team, Warrener said the team surprised in their first year, finishing seventh overall. "It was way beyond anyone's expectation," he said, so he felt he was joining a team on the right track.

The team had enough veterans—goaltender John Vanbiesbrouck and forwards Dave Lowry and Brian Skrudland—who refused to lose on a fledgling team. "They may have went in the expansion draft but they were still capable of playing and being effective," he said. "But it was still a surprise for Florida to be that good."

Warrener said he appreciated the veteran influence on the Panthers, but by the time he laced up his skates with the team in their third year, they were already shifting gears toward more youth with the likes of Rob Niedermayer and Ed Jovanovski as the team's future.

Still, Warrener said as he joined the team his ice time was more limited than it might have been—he played in only 28 games his first year—as the team tried to determine the direction it was going. "I didn't get into as many games as they expected," he said. That became a real positive in his hockey career, as it allowed him to join Team Canada for the World Junior Championships held in Boston in 1996. "We had a real good team. We had a lot of good players," he said, noting the team would win the gold medal, stretching Canada's run of golds to five consecutive years.

Warrener said while he didn't get to travel to an exotic locale for the Championships, Boston was great because so many Canadian fans were able to attend games.

Of course winning the gold medal also stands out in his career. "The gold was pretty special," he said, but added he still wants a Stanley Cup knowing that will be sweeter too, especially after the run with Calgary. "The Stanley Cup is what everyone dreams about."

Warrener made a run at the Cup with the Panthers, making it to the finals, and then the team switched gears, trading emerging stars such as Jovanovski, which sent the message no one was safe. That would include Warrener, who was sent to Buffalo part way through the 1998—99 season. "Florida got rid of a lot of guys," he said, adding the move was not a bad one for his career.

In fact, in four-and-a-half seasons in Buffalo, Warrener would go to the finals, and again see a team shift gears and move in a new direction with its personnel. It was in the change over that Warrener ended up a Flame, the team he is most well know for playing with in this country after its Cup run.

It has also been an opportunity for Warrener to play with Jarome Iginla, one of the best of the current era in the NHL. "All-around he's just a special guy from being an amazing hockey player, to the way he lives his life, to the way everyone respects him."

Warrener said Iginla earns his respect by his work ethic, and the fact he does whatever is needed to succeed. For example, while often told as a big-time scorer he shouldn't fight, Warrener said, "that's just his nature to win the battles, and to do everything in his power to win."

Now the goal is another visit to the finals, with hopefully a ring at the end of the run. He added he hopes to play at least 15 years in the NHL. If that doesn't happen, Warrener has already eclipsed 500 career games in the NHL, and has enjoyed long playoff runs in three cities. It's a career he is proud of.

"I like to think it's just an example of hard work, and how that can pay off. My belief is you always go out and give it everything you can."

An Excellent Back-Up

When it comes to coaching, few can match the successful numbers Doug Sauter has amassed in more than 30 years behind the bench as a professional. Sauter, who grew up in Fairlight, Saskatchewan, was relaxing in his hotel room in Memphis the day he was interviewed. "If we win tonight it will be my 1,100th win as a head coach," he said Jan. 28. "I don't know of many guys that have won that many." It would be Sauter's milestone victory later that day as his Oklahoma City Blazers defeated the Memphis River Kings 4-2.

The wins for Sauter have rolled up over the years—his biggest accomplishment occurred December 26, 2003, in Lubbock, Texas. The Blazers 4–1 win over the Lubbock Cotton Kings was Doug's 1,000th victory as a head coach. While aware of the milestones, he said it's not something he dwells on as highly important either. "I don't know if they're really important to me, it's kind of for perseverance and longevity, and I think that's important to anybody, whether you're a farmer or businessman, doing something you're proud of."

Growing up in Fairlight Sauter said his memories are certainly those of hockey, and as teenager of only 14 or 15 he left home to pursue the game. He was a goaltender who would play first in Unity, then on to North Battleford, where he first tasted real success as a member of the Beaver Bruins. "We won a Juvenile "A" Championship that year," he recalled.

By the age of 19, Sauter was playing in Bellingham, Washington, and he would get his first taste of drawing the Xs and Os of the game, acting as a playing assistant coach.

However, his first coaching experience was short-lived, as he moved on to Calgary in the WCHL for the 1972–73 season. "I played two games. My back-up was John Davidson [now a familiar TV commentator]. He played in '63," joked Sauter.

Sauter said he fully appreciates "my playing career was not great." In fact, he calls himself an excellent back-up. "I was a very good back-up goaltender. I considered myself a hard worker. I never worried about my ice time. I did what I could to help the team, any way I could."

While not a great netminder, Sauter did get a tryout in the Boston Bruin organization. "I ended up in Dayton for a while," he said, but the stay was short-lived. Tom McClelland with the New Westminster Bruins called the 20-year-old goaltender and offered him a position as assistant coach to Bill Shinske. Sauter said yes. "It was the best thing I ever did."

Looking back, Sauter said the call from the Bruins opened the doors on a new career. "I never wanted to be a coach when I was young, but when the decision was made that I wasn't good enough to play…I was very lucky to get the opportunity."

In New Westminster Sauter learned from the bottom up, doing everything from delivering tickets, to sharpening skates and collecting jerseys. "I never went to formal university, but I went to Bruins University and learned my trade. I can never repay those two guys [McClelland and Shinske]. Those are the guys that gave me a life in hockey."

In four seasons under coach Shinske, Sauter and the Bruins would go to the Memorial Cup each season, winning twice. "It was very exciting. We won the league four years in a row. We went to the Memorial Cup four years. We definitely had a dynasty those four years."

One player stands out in Sauter's mind from his time as the Bruins assistant: Stan Smyl, who would go on to a 13 year career with the Vancouver Canucks. "He played all four years. I don't think anybody else can say they went to four Memorial Cups," said Sauter.

With the success as a Bruin assistant coach on the resume, Sauter said "it was time to move on and become a head coach myself."

Sauter may have left the Bruins after four seasons, but he would become a fixture in the Western Hockey League for the next 17 seasons, rolling up 417 wins with Calgary, Brandon, Regina and Medicine Hat. Although he never enjoyed the success of Memorial Cup victory like he did in New Westminster, he also never had a losing season. "I never won the league, but we went to the finals a couple of times," he said. Not winning was a disappointment in the sense "you always want to win the big one."

With Calgary Sauter came close. "We lost in the seventh game in probably one of the most exciting games I ever coached in," he said. The two teams sported a couple of goaltenders destined for National Hockey League greatness. "Grant Fuhr was in net for them [Victoria], and Mike Vernon was my goalie. They scored with three minutes left to win it."

Sauter said Vernon was among many great players he coached. "He was one of the guys that had a great career and won a Stanley Cup."

While coming close in the WHL, in 1989 when he was coaching in Brandon, it looked like his coaching career might come to an end when he contracted Guillain-Barré syndrome. "Guillain-Barré syndrome is an acute illness involving the peripheral nervous system that usually occurs two to three weeks after a flu-like disease or other infections. It is mostly a motor neuropathy, meaning that its symptoms are largely related to the involvement of the motor nerves," explained a website on the disease.

The disease took Sauter away from the Brandon bench, and it marked the only season where his team had a sub-.500 record, although he missed most of the action. "For the whole year [1990] I didn't coach," said Sauter.

When Sauter had recovered he chose to move on to the professional ranks south of the border as a coach, although he admitted the decision was not an easy one. "Without a doubt. I'm a firm believer, and firm supporter of the WHL."

Sauter had his pro coaching debut in Winston-Salem of the East Coast Hockey League. He would spend four seasons in the ECHL, the last three with the Wheeling Thunderbirds. Then it was on to the Oklahoma City Blazers of the Central Hockey League for the 1995–96 season. For the next eight years he would lead the team to the playoffs, missing for the first time in 2004. "We were still over .500 but didn't make it." It was his first year with the Blazers to register less than 35 wins. Along the way he became the winningest coach in CHL history.

After some 30 years as coach Sauter faced an unusual situation in the 2004–05 season. "This year we're below .500. I'm having a tough time with it actually. We've lost 20 games by one goal, seven in overtime," he said. "...It's frustrating a year like this. You question yourself—have I coached enough? Is it something I'm doing wrong?"

Still, the Blazers have been a good fit for Sauter, who said he loves the city, and appreciates the city's surprisingly long hockey history. "There's lot of tradition here. The Blazers have been around for a long time. Harry Sinden [famous with Boston in the NHL] was a player coach here," he said. He added the likes of Glen Sather, Terry Crisp, Gerry Cheevers, Dallas Smith and Ross Lonsberry all made stops with the Blazers during their careers.

Fans too appreciate hockey, even in a city with great college football and basketball programs, said Sauter. "In my 10 years we've led all of minor hockey in attendance," he said, adding crowds are regularly in excess of 9,000.

Sauter seems to have found a permanent home in Oklahoma City, a city he recalls arriving at during a very solemn time. On April 1995, at 9:02, a van packed with home-made explosives and parked outside the Alfred P. Murrah federal building in downtown Oklahoma City exploded.

Half of the nine-story building collapsed, killing 168 people, including 19 children, and injuring more than 500 others, making it the most deadly peacetime attack on U.S. soil to that date.

It was into the solemn atmosphere of post-bombing Oklahoma City that Sauter arrived as coach. "Not a lot of people in Oklahoma City felt very good about themselves," he recalled. In his first season Sauter led the team to the Adams Cup for best regular season record, and then the Levins Trophy playoff championship, earning him Coach of the Year honours. The championship came almost a year to the date of the bombing. "That made a lot of people feel good about themselves again." Sauter said it was one of those events in hockey, where he realized the connection the game can have to life.

More recently, Sauter said he had one of those moments where he recognized too that there are larger things than hockey, even if at times you're focused on the game. He said he was watching television as he was doing some paperwork. There was a TV spot talking about one of the American soldiers who had died in Iraq. "There I was worried about my power play, and there was a guy that just gave his life to protect our freedom. So how important is my power play in terms of other things?"

Sauter said that while careers are measured in successes, he sees a picture bigger than solely measuring success in terms of hockey. "Hockey isn't always about wins and losses. It isn't always about goals and assists. It's about life." That point was driven home while Sauter coached Brad Hornung with the Regina Pats in his WHL days. "He went through the worst accident you can go through. The only thing worse would be to have died, and he's still going strong. He's a role model. Of all the guys I've coached in hockey, he is the one that showed the most guts."

It was a game against the Moose Jaw Warriors, the Pats long-time rivals. In the intensity of the contest, Hornung was driving to the net when Moose Jaw's Troy Edwards gave him an extra shove from behind. The momentum of the push took Hornung past the net and into the boards head first, damaging Hornung's third cervical vertebra and spinal cord. The accident left Hornung paralyzed from the neck down and unable to move any of his extremities.

For Sauter the turn to coaching has fit him like a glove, and his record speaks for itself. "It's given me the opportunity to do something that I love, and be involved in the game I love," he said. At the same time coaching over three decades has meant he has had to adapt his style at times. "My style has kind of changed over the years. There's a reason for my long moustache. Sometimes I have to bite my lip under here," he said with a chuckle.

One thing that hasn't altered over the years is his competitive spirit. "I love to win. It doesn't matter what I do in life. I love to win at golf, at cards, at hockey," he said. Still, Sauter tries to stay constant in some of his coaching philosophies through the years. "Never ask a player to do something you wouldn't do yourself," he said.

While he has had to change his approach as a coach, Sauter said players too have changed. "The biggest thing, all players have more options now. Hockey isn't the main thing anymore. They have all kinds of other options they can do," he said.

"Players are far more knowledgeable now. From websites a player can find out information on any team, any player in a matter of minutes." It's the same for the coach too. "After a game, within 20 minutes I can know every score of every professional game in the United States and Canada, and who scored the goals, and who's been put on waivers, and who's been traded."

When it comes to picking players off the wire, or from camps, Sauter said he looks beyond the numbers. "I'll give up a little bit of talent to get somebody who has a great attitude, and has a great work ethic," he said. "...The big thing is I've always been more about character and work ethic. It's more important to be the best person you can be than being the absolute best hockey player."

Sauter said he's as proud of the players he has coached who have gone on to have good lives after hockey, as he is of the players who put up great professional careers.

In his pro career Sauter has obviously done well, actually avoiding a fate almost every coach faces at least once. "I've never been fired, but I knew when to move a couple of times," he said with a chuckle.

It is unlikely he'll be fired now, as he looks at Oklahoma City as being his last stop as a coach. "I don't plan on going anywhere else...I'll know when it's over, when I'm not excited and I'm not keyed up about the game anymore," he said, adding he's never aspired to coach in the NHL. "If you coach in the NHL you have to think about nothing but hockey. I've always liked having other interests. It's made my life more diverse. I wouldn't want to think nothing but hockey 24/7, 365 days a year," he said.

"The only thing I ever missed from the NHL is a bigger pay cheque, and if I was only coaching for the money I don't think it would have been the same...The way it is, I love it, I just absolutely love it."

The Moosomin Moose—Playing for Time

Imagine a hockey game where the score ended up 97-83, and the players were all smiles at the outcome.

Imagine that the next time the two teams faced off, the score was again close, but the score bloated to 429–414, followed by yet a third match-up where the score ended 1125–1111. The games in question were all played by the Moosomin Moose as they attempted to set Guinness Book of World Record marks, while at the same time raising money for a new hospital in the town.

"We were meeting down in one of the fellas' basements and the idea came up," said Dave Towler, who played in the first game. Mike Schwean, who played in all three games, is credited with the idea, although he said his first thoughts weren't of playing three marathon games, but simply to find a suitable fundraising project for the recreational Moose team to undertake.

"We kind of talked about it. We did some looking through the Guinness Book, but there wasn't much in there," he said. "We weren't really sure what they wanted for a record." So they contacted the office of Guinness in Britain and were told anything over 20 hours would set the mark.

The idea of using the game as a catalyst to raise money was simple enough: play hockey for 26 hours, set a record, and with luck raise $10 to $15,000 for the hospital fund. "The hospital funding, nothing had been happening for awhile," said Towler. "We thought maybe we could kick-start it, and get it going again."

Towler said the idea was to have each of the 40 players raise pledges, each collecting at least $250, just to play, and they'd raise the $10,000. "It just really took off from there."

Finding players to take on a game that would extend more than 24 hours proved relatively easy. "The first game was pretty good. We had a real good nucleus of players [on the Moose]," said Towler, who added that players came from three other recreational teams in the town, and from the surrounding area to flesh out the rosters. "With the goal to raise money for the hospital, it wasn't hard to twist their arms."

Training for the game, held November 23 and 24 in 2001, was left to the bravado of jocks, admitted Fowler, who said the players basically felt they "were young enough and foolish enough" to play the extended game. "Some of the guys went to the gym. For most of us, the ice was just basically being put in, so we'd played a game or two."

Raising money remained the primary goal, and raise money they did, eclipsing their goals some tenfold. By the time the game was complete, the Moose had played for 25 hours, 10 minutes and raised $125,000. "It caught on like wild fire," said Towler.

However, the game didn't set the record with Guinness. "We were a bit misinformed," said Towler. Only two weeks earlier a girls' team in British Columbia had eclipsed their mark before the Moose even hit the ice.

Towler said participating in the game was a thrill. "It was a great feeling. All the camaraderie in the dressing room—everybody was so energized."

The game was tiring, too. "It was really tough," said Towler. "Everybody was on the bench for every period. It was really difficult sitting on the wooden benches that long."

The players did get regular intermission breaks, which included food and refreshments prepared by volunteers, but that was the only break.

With no naps and no opportunity for gear to dry out, it was tough, agreed Schwean. "You never really took your skates off the whole time. There were a lot of guys with blisters. We got a lot smarter the second time around."

The toughest role fell to the netminders. Going in, they agreed four hours was about the maximum they could play at one time, but even as they switched off, it didn't afford much recuperation time by the time a goalie stripped his gear and tried to relax.

Towler said the feeling of the game was amazing. When Premier Lorne Calvert spoke at centre ice, "it was special realizing what we had done."

Towler said the initial game stuck to hockey more than the later marathons. "It was a more realistic hockey game. The only breaks were when the Zamboni cleaned the ice."

The two teams also wanted to win the marathon. "That first game there was a little bit of a competitive edge in everybody. The teams never let up once in 25 hours. There was no lolly-gagging around."

So the 25-hour hockey game was a winner in fundraising, but the Moose name was still not in the Guinness Book of World Records. The solution was simply do it again. The Moose hit the ice January 9 to 12, 2003, this time raising the bar on ice time. The two teams squared off for 62 hours, 15 minutes.

Towler explained Guinness had relaxed its rules following

the first game, allowing for part of the team not to be on the bench. "So we had all the extra dressing rooms set up with cots." The game was bolstered by Sheldon Kennedy, a former NHLer from nearby Manitoba, showing up to play.

The atmosphere on the ice was more focused on just keeping the game going. "They had to look after themselves, and pace themselves," said Towler, who was shelved by a bad back for the game.

Schwean said the game, and the longer one yet to follow, were grinds. "It's funny, different guys hit the wall at different times, but there always seemed at least one guy was still going hard and doing something silly to keep everybody else going."

This time, as the hours climbed, so did donations for the hospital, raising $205,000. The game also got the Moose into the 2004 Guinness Book of World Records, although it was a short-lived crown.

So, the Moose went at it one more time October 13 to 18, 2003, playing for 130 hours, seven minutes. Again support blossomed, raising $175,000 for the hospital.

This time another former NHLer, Jeff Odgers, joined the Moose for the game. Schwean said Odgers knows only one way to play, and that's hard, and he basically played himself out to the point where he stayed off skates for several weeks after the contest.

Schwean said over the three games, not one player ever stepped away from the ice. One was cut badly, and returned after stitches. Another played much of a game with a broken finger. And a girl—Kayla Mannle—playing in the longest game twisted an ankle and should have retired but didn't. "She should have quit. She missed a big part of her season after that and still feels it," said Schwean.

"It was pretty bad," admitted Mannle of the injury. "They still don't know what's wrong with it. I don't know what I did to it, but it still bothers me."

Still, hanging up the skates and not finishing the game was not on the then 16-year-old Mannle's agenda. "I got some needles and kept playing. It was a big deal being the only girl to have participated in a game like that [at the time]," she said. "I knew I wanted to finish. I didn't think about quitting."

Other than the ankle, Mannle, who has played hockey since she was old enough to skate, said the game was not as hard as she had expected. "I thought it would be harder than it was," she said. "It was as much fun as I thought it would be."

Again the game set a Guinness record, but Towler said a team in Guelph appears to have eclipsed the mark, although that is not yet official from Guinness.

As long as the game was, and players knowing they needed to pace themselves, there was still a desire to win. "By the nature of the beast it's competitive. It's hard to get away from that," said Schwean.

Towler said there are no plans to attack the record a fourth time. "There's no more," he said. "We're very satisfied with what we've done here."

Schwean isn't so sure the gas tank is empty for the Moose. "I was the one who wanted the second and third games. I wouldn't count us out just yet," he said. It may be a year or so into the future, as much to let the town regenerate to support the fundraising side of the game, as to let the players ready themselves for yet another marathon.

While other teams have perhaps racked up more on-ice hours, Towler said it's the fundraising, over half a million in the three games, the Moose are most proud of. "The other teams don't come close in fundraising."

Towler said the success is because of the volunteers who helped look after the players, verified all the requirements listed by Guinness and helped raise funds. "Once it was announced we were going to do this, everybody was asking 'what can we do to help?'"

Schwean agreed volunteers were a huge part of the success, from helping keep the players comfortable, to making sure the documentation to satisfy Guinness was maintained, to running parallel fundraising events such as pancake breakfasts and cabarets. "It was probably easier to play the game than do all the other stuff," he said with a chuckle.

As for the hospital, it remains a dream for the community. "Land has been purchased. Money has been promised. We're hoping sod is turned early this summer [2005]," said Towler. "So the light is getting brighter at the end of the tunnel."

A Team Player

Anytime you play more than one thousand games in the National Hockey League, you've put together an amazing career. For Brad McCrimmon it sort of mimics the name of the small Saskatchewan town where he grew up and learned the game—the town of Plenty.

While it has been a lot of years and a ton of NHL miles since McCrimmon learned to play in Plenty, it was there that the basics of the game were set—helped along by a family long focused on hockey. "Dad coached and played in [nearby] Rosetown for the Rosetown Red Wings for a number of years," he said. "… It was always talk of farming or hockey at our kitchen table."

With a tie to Rosetown, McCrimmon found himself travelling to play with teams there at a young age, while still skating on the natural ice with teams in Plenty. The doubling up of game time at an early age was a definite bonus something he said is missing with rule changes these days.

In his day McCrimmon said it wasn't that unusual to play for your hometown, and then for a larger community nearby. Now players are usually restricted to one team, and that can be bad news for the game in smaller towns. "If a couple of players go to play in a larger centre, you don't have enough kids sometimes in the small towns," he said. He reasoned it would be better to allow players with skills to step up to a higher level by travelling, but still be able to support the game at home.

McCrimmon was also doubling up on games as a kid, playing a lot of games for teams above his normal age category. He said as a Pee Wee he was also playing on a Bantam team, and as a Bantam was getting a taste of Midget. It was hockey development on the fast track, and one he said was great for those ready to handle it.

In McCrimmon's case he handled it with ease and by the time he was 15 and 16 he was playing Junior Tier II with the Prince Albert Raiders. "It was a good environment and culture to play Tier II in." In Prince Albert, McCrimmon came under the guidance of coach Terry Simpson, one of the more respected coaches of his era. "He was a no-nonsense guy and a straight-up guy. He expected you to work hard and know the basics of the game."

Years later, after 18 seasons and 1,222 regular season games, McCrimmon himself would move behind the bench as a coach, and he admitted little things he learned from coaches such as Simpson became part of his own philosophy. "You carry little things from every coach you play for," he said.

But, McCrimmon said the real foundation for a coach comes from his earliest days simply growing up on a farm in Saskatchewan. "When you're growing up on the family farm with grandma and grandpa and mom and dad, that's where you learn all things about life that become your base... You take little pieces of these people with you."

On the ice, McCrimmon also experienced a taste of success

as a Raider. "My second year we went to the western finals. We lost to Spruce Grove. The first year we were in the provincial final."

While the Raiders were right on the edge of big things to come—they would win four of the next six Centennial Cup Championships—McCrimmon decided to move on, joining the Brandon Wheat Kings of the Western Hockey League. "I always wanted to play in the Western League and at that time I was on the Brandon list."

It was an easy team to join, as the Wheat Kings were a league powerhouse at the time. "It still goes down as one of the best teams ever," said McCrimmon, pointing to a streak without a loss set in 1979 that took until the fall of 2004 to be broken by the London Knights. It was a streak stretching over 56 games, if you include overlapping seasons, he added.

Dunc McCallum was coach in Brandon, and he proved to be another person whose style McCrimmon would draw on as a coach himself. "He was innovative enough to all that team [Wheat Kings] to grow and mature."

At the time Brandon was deep in talent, led by a potent offence including Brian Propp, Ray Allison and Laurie Boschman. McCrimmon himself flirted with 100-point seasons from his spot on the blueline all three seasons in Brandon as well.

"It was a pretty dynamic team for sure," he said. Even 26 years later he stays in contact with some members of the team, although time has broken many of the ties. "But I can still look at a team picture and remember every guy, and things about that season."

Still, the big prize of the Memorial Cup eluded McCrimmon and the Wheat Kings. After posting a 58–5–9 record during the regular season, they defeated Portland in six games to capture the team's first-ever President's Cup. Brandon finished the three-team round robin with a 2–3–0 record. The Wheat Kings then dropped the sudden death final 2–1 to the Peterborough Petes in overtime.

Although the Memorial Cup was not in the cards, McCrimmon's personal play made him a first round draft choice of the Boston Bruins in 1979, going 15th overall.

The draft in 1979 was exciting for McCrimmon and his family, but not quite the media spectacle it has become today. "There wasn't the hype and the build-up there is today. I was working on the swather getting ready to go to the field when I got the call."

The call was rather short and sweet too, suggesting the Bruins would send the new draftee "some information," then adding, "we'll see you in camp."

McCrimmon's selection by the Bruins was not a surprise, but a welcome occurrence. "They'd called about a week before the draft and asked a couple of questions, so I knew they had some interest."

For a young player from Plenty, it was a huge step to his first National Hockey League training camp in Boston, but again a step he took in stride. The first camp was a tight group, with just a few players more than the roster limited to the Bruins and their minor league affiliate. "I started in the farm team room."

But sometimes fate plays a card for young players, and it seemed it was dealing aces for McCrimmon. Bruin defencemen Brad Park and Gary Doak both suffered injuries that kept them out of the lineup until Christmas. "It was an opportunity to stay in Boston. The injuries were a major factor in that."

At the same time, McCrimmon said he headed to the first Boston camp expecting to emerge wearing a Bruins jersey. "I guess I was so green, young and naive, but I went there thinking I was going to be playing for the Bruins. I left home thinking I'm going to be playing for the Bruins this year."

The Boston team McCrimmon joined was one deep in talent, including the likes of gritty captain Terry O'Reilley, as well as Wayne Cashman, Jean Ratelle and netminder Gerry Cheevers.

Ray Bourque also joined the Bruins that same year, having been drafted ahead of McCrimmon.

So when the dust of camp settled, McCrimmon stayed with the big club, and would never spend time in the minors over 18 pro seasons to follow. When he played his first game with the Bruins, it was the first time he'd seen an NHL game, getting more of a bird's eye view than most seeing their first pro game. "I'd never seen a pro game in person until I played one," he said. As a youth teams in Winnipeg, Edmonton and Calgary weren't yet in the NHL to make it easier for a family from Saskatchewan to take in a game.

McCrimmon said he recalls one game early in his career in particular, where Jean Ratelle took a high stick, something unusual for a player so respected for his demeanor and style on the ice. "Stan Jonathan proceeded to go over and have quite a physical discussion with the gentleman who did it," he said.

McCrimmon would have a solid rookie season, and continue to progress in his second season in Boston, but the third year was less impressive, and the Bruins made a move. He was sent to Philadelphia for netminder Pete Peeters, a move McCrimmon said he understood as making good hockey sense. "Boston was having trouble in goal and were desperate for a goaltender, and Pete Peeters was a good fit," he said. The Bruins had also drafted rearguard Gord Kluzak, a solid replacement for his spot in the roster.

On the positive side for McCrimmon was the fact he was rejoining two old Brandon teammates in Philadelphia: Brian Propp and Ray Allison. "It's always good to walk into a dressing room as a new guy and see some familiar faces," he said.

Again, the Flyers were a good team, just a shade short of Stanley Cup glory. "My five years in Philly, we had a really good team," said McCrimmon. "My career continued to grow there. I had some opportunities that I took advantage of."

McCrimmon said that's always a key for any player. When chances occur to play on the power play, get more ice time or to evolve into a more important role with a team, a player must be ready to grasp the opportunity.

In Philly, McCrimmon was playing for one of the most notorious coaches in recent memory, Mike Keenan, yet he never ran afoul of the spirited coach, and he learned things too. "He's a black and white guy. If you did your job, and worked hard every night, you never had any trouble with Mike."

It was Keenan who provided the opportunity of teaming with Mark Howe for a defensive pairing during his final three seasons as a Flyer. "That was a pretty successful partnership," said McCrimmon. It was a partnership which came with the fringe benefit of getting to know Mark's father, the legendary Gordie Howe. "I got to spend some Christmases with Mark, and his mom and dad would show up," he said.

There was also an invitation to go fishing with Mark, along with Howe's brother Marty and some of their friends. McCrimmon accepted. "I get to the Virgin Islands and Gordie's there too. Here I am blue marlin fishing with Gordie Howe. Where I come from, spending a week with Gordie Howe is like spending a week with God."

As a Flyer McCrimmon also came close to a Stanley Cup, losing in seven games to Edmonton. He still marks the loss as a career highlight. "After the game in the dressing room, looking at every player, you knew no one cheated or didn't do their absolute best to win. We didn't have an ounce left. We just couldn't beat the Edmonton Oilers. As disappointing at that was, I still look back on it with pride."

McCrimmon's tenure in Philadelphia would end after five seasons. This time McCrimmon was on his way to Calgary, and three seasons with the Flames. The highlight of that time was the

Stanley Cup ring which came in 1989. "You never replace that," he said. The Flames had a team deep in dedicated players, such as Doug Gilmour, Gary Roberts and Lanny McDonald. "It was a really unique bunch of players."

In McDonald the Flames had a "rallying point" in its run to the Cup, since the long-time player had never earned one. Of course McCrimmon too wanted the ring badly, having been to the finals before, but not winning.

As sweet as the Stanley Cup was, McCrimmon said he appreciated playing in Calgary because he was finally playing close enough to home for friends and family to attend games. "All my friends from Plenty who I grew up with had families by then, and they'd come down and I'd take them on dressing room tours, or if Edmonton was in town get them pictures with Wayne Gretzky. It was a great experience."

Three seasons in Calgary and the experience was over. McCrimmon moved to Detroit, and initially that meant mixed feelings. "They had been a sub-.500 team for a long time, and not a very pretty team." But the year McCrimmon arrived, they came close to the .500 mark, and in the spring of 1991, "came within a whisker of upsetting St. Louis," who finished some 30 points higher in the standings. "The next two years we were over 100 points," said McCrimmon.

To be on the Wings as they re-established past glory in the NHL was an accomplishment McCrimmon was proud of. "Anytime you can be part of a team that moves forward, it's great, and not only did we move forward, we took some great strides."

As the Wings readied to take the final steps to Stanley Cup glory, McCrimmon was moved yet again, heading to Hartford. "When I got there we had some good players like Sean Burke and Geoff Sanderson and Andrew Cassels. But we didn't have enough depth to survive injuries," he said. A key player would end up on the shelf, and the Whalers would stumble. They finished fifth in their conference during McCrimmon's first season.

As a veteran, McCrimmon was pragmatic about his time in Hartford. "I was there to try and make them better, I wasn't sitting there crying in my milk."

Then there was one more move for McCrimmon, who signed with Phoenix as a free agent in 1996. It was the Coyotes first year after moving from Winnipeg. "Mom and Dad spent winters down there, so in my 18th year they got to watch me," he said.

An injury shortened his season in Phoenix, and after the year, his career was over. "As a player you like to think you'll never retire, but unfortunately the time comes when you just don't have it," he said. "I'd have liked to have played another 10 years, but my day had come."

McCrimmon didn't stay away from the NHL for long. The fall after his retirement as a player he was behind the bench as assistant coach with the New York Islanders. The move wasn't a huge surprise, considering he had been a player mentor in his final years for younger players such as Gary Suter, Chris Pronger and Nicklas Lidstrom.

Now settled into a career as a coach, McCrimmon said he likes how the position keeps him in the game at a top level. "I enjoy it immensely. You're still part of the game, can smell it, hear the sounds. You're right down where the action is."

Coaching also keeps McCrimmon in hockey. "I just love everything about the game," he said. He doesn't look at his career in terms of numbers, but rather in terms of a great opportunity and experience. "I don't remember playing a thousandth game or 18 years. I was never an individual numbers things. I was a team player."

The Vancouver Connection

Orland Kurtenbach may have grown up along the first fringe of Saskatchewan, learning to play hockey in Prince Albert, but it is Vancouver he will forever be associated with.

Born on a farm near Cudworth, Kurtenbach's family made a couple of moves before settling in Prince Albert. "I really didn't start playing hockey until I got to Prince Albert," he explained. Having not played the game or barely skated before, he was a step behind most kids his age. "The first time I tried out for a team, I didn't make it." Being cut wasn't a deterrent for the young forward. He would keep working at the game, and by the spring of 1950, would be on a championship Bantam team.

As Kurtenbach developed, he found himself, like a lot of talented youngsters of his day, playing at levels higher than his own age group. In fact, as a Midget he played half a season of senior hockey, an opportunity he said clearly made him better. "That really toughened me up, and knocked me on my can a few times."

He played his Junior in Prince Albert and in four seasons recorded 321 points, averaging 37 goals and 43 assists a season or 2 points a game. He also shone in the Saskatchewan Junior Hockey League with the Mintos. Along the way he made his presence felt as a tenacious checker. Kurtenbach also had a cup of coffee in the old Western Hockey League with the Saskatoon Quakers, and then came one of those rare opportunities to play for all the marbles.

The opportunity came through a playoff pick-up by the Flin Flon Bombers in 1957, along with Jean Gauthier from Lakehead. "I played with Flin Flon when they beat Hull-Ottawa," said Kurtenbach. At that time Flin Flon was a strong team, bringing in a lot of players who found jobs at the local mine, giving them lucrative wage packages as a lure to play for the Bombers. "They always had good clubs, but hadn't won the Memorial Cup. The year they did win it, there were about seven players right from Flin Flon on the team." The Bomber roster included future NHLers such as Teddy Hampson, Duane Rupp, Mel Pearson and George Konik.

Kurtenbach said the team they faced from Hull-Ottawa was one deep in talent. They were Montreal's top Junior team, the Hull-Ottawa Canadians, a Canadian All Star team managed by future Montreal General Manager Sam Pollock and coached by Scotty Bowman, who is wisely considered the best coach in National Hockey League history. Hull-Ottawa also had a roster of stars including Murray Balfour, Ralph Backstrom, Claude Ruel, Claude Dufour and Billy Carter.

The Bombers were decided underdogs, but the series was in the west, although Flin Flon hosted only three games because their arena was small, so the rest of the series was played in Regina.

The Bombers won two-of-three in their home arena, but Hull-Ottawa rebounded to win the next two and lead the series 3–2. The Bombers won the next game, to force a sudden death seventh meeting, a game that Flin Flon would take. Kurtenbach played a key checking role, especially in the third, giving the Bombers their only Memorial Cup victory in the team's history. "It was an unbelievable place to play and win it," said Kurtenbach, who added Flin Flon is an amazing place to play hockey because of its raucous fans.

By the fall of the Memorial Cup season, Kurtenbach would turn pro, joining the Vancouver Canucks of the old Western Hockey League, a farm team of the New York Rangers at the time. Although he had no way of knowing, it would be the start of a long circular path through professional hockey. Kurtenbach admitted Vancouver was a cultural jump, as well as a step in hockey, for a player who had grown up in the game in Prince Albert. "It was a big adjustment, but you have to take things in stride," he said. The biggest thing was dealing with players far more experienced at that level than he was.

It was certainly a solid first stride for Kurtenbach, as he scored 54 points in 52 games and was named the Coast Division rookie of the year in the WHL.

In the spring of 1958, Kurtenbach took another step, being one of three Canucks moved to the Buffalo Bisons of the American Hockey League by the parent Rangers.

One of the more interesting games in Kurtenbach's career occurred with the Bisons in the spring of 1959. It was near the end of the season, and the Bisons were in a meaningless game with Rochester.

Buffalo's only goalie, Marcel Paille, got hit between the eyes in the last minute of the first period, recalled Kurtenbach. "Doug Barkley and I were used sparingly, so when Marcel got hit and our practice goalie from Fort Erie did not make the game, Fred Hunt our GM asked jokingly for volunteers," he said. "I went in."

The contest had another Saskatchewan connection Kurtenbach still remembers too. Another Saskatchewan player and

SJHL rival, Bill Hicke, was the leading scorer in the American League and needed to record two points to set a league record. "I had a great time as Bill Hicke was going for the rookie goal scoring title of 44 goals, which was held by a Buffalo teammate Wally Hergesheimer at 43," said Kurtenbach, who recalled allowing five goals in about 30 shots.

Still, for the first time, Kurtenbach didn't like the move up in hockey. "I wasn't playing very much, and I wasn't very happy," he said. The move to Springfield was the last straw, and he asked for a ticket back to Vancouver. "Springfield went on to win about three championships in a row, but I came back to Vancouver."

Kurtenbach felt more at home in the WHL with the Canucks. "The Western League was more of a family-oriented league. There was a lot of travelling by car, and the families came along," he said. That was important to him since he had married a West Coast girl. "I enjoyed the Western Hockey League. I enjoyed the West Coast."

Finally, he would move up to the NHL. He played his first games—10 that season—with the Rangers in 1960–61, and would then be traded to the Boston Bruins, finally getting a real NHL shot with the start of the 1963 season, when he played in 70 games.

Between 1963 and 1965 Kurtenbach saw full-time duty with the Bruins, playing on a line with Dean Prentice and Andy Hebenton, before being traded to Toronto for a season, and back to the Rangers for four.

His career to that point was solid, but always something short of expectation, often owing to a back injury incurred in Boston breaking in a new pair of skates. "Every year, a couple of times a season, my back would tighten up, and I couldn't do anything at all," he said.

There were also times Kurtenbach didn't like the role he

was cast in. In Toronto, for example, coach Punch Imlach wanted him to concentrate solely on defence. "I didn't like that at all," said Kurtenbach, who had always had some success around the net, having had a trio of 35-plus points seasons in the NHL.

At least in New York things turned better under coach Emile "Cat" Francis. "I got a lot of ice time until my back started to act up again," said Kurtenbach.

In New York, Kurtenbach would have the old injury treated through an operation by Dr. Yanagasawa. "For me it was a real saviour," he said, adding his career was extended by the back fusion operation. The third, fourth and fifth vertebra were notched to make way for a rectangular bone removed from Kurtenbach's left hip. After the operation, for six months he wore a stainless steel corset covering from his chest to over his hips when out of bed. Other Rangers to be operated on by Dr. Yanagasawa were Jean Ratelle, Rod Gilbert, Harry Howell and Camille Henry.

Still, Kurtenbach had been out of the game for nearly two years through the operation, and was an unknown quantity in light of the surgery, so was left unprotected in the expansion draft which saw Vancouver and Buffalo join the NHL. "I knew I was going to either Buffalo or Vancouver," he said, adding being left unprotected was not a surprise.

Given his connections to Vancouver, Kurtenbach was happy it was the Canucks who selected him. "It was electric. As soon as the draft was over, we were packed and ready to move."

Kurtenbach was named the team's first Captain, and said he simply soaked in the extraordinary atmosphere of that first season. "I got off to a great start, and the hockey club was doing very well." The start for Kurtenbach included the team's first hat trick December 12, 1970, in a 5–2 victory over the visiting California Seals. "There was an excitement in the city just being in the NHL, and we were in a playoff position too."

Veteran players such as Ted Taylor and Murray Hall, Bobby Schmautz, goaltender Charlie Hodge and Dunc Wilson, with younger additions such as Pat Quinn and Rosaire Paiement, helped the team win 24 games that first season. Kurtenbach said for an expansion team, the Canucks had surprising grit and confidence. "Nobody was too concerned even going into a rink like Philadelphia. We did what we had to do, and weren't intimidated a bit."

The Canucks might have done better that first year if not for the dreaded road schedule of a West Coast franchise. "We had road trips of 10 days, even one that was 14 days. We'd played a three-game or five-game road trip, get back to Vancouver Monday and have to play Tuesday. You were walking in a fog. It was just awful.

"It wasn't just the games, it was the waiting around at the friggin' airports. You would be coming out of Chicago to Seattle then wait two or three hours for a half-hour flight into Vancouver."

The fatigue factor is all it takes at the NHL level, where one goal is often the difference. "That physical tiredness leads to those mental mistakes on the ice," said Kurtenbach. "Against good teams, that one mental lapse and it was over."

The travel has never changed for teams like Vancouver, but Kurtenbach looks back on that expansion team and believes it could have developed into a true contender, except for one thing—the arrival of the World Hockey Association. While he credits the WHA with dragging NHL salaries closer to those of other professional sports, it did steal several players from the Canucks, who didn't have the organizational depth to fill the holes. "It got the NHL out of the doldrums of paying $20,000 or $30,000, but it really hurt our hockey club. We lost the likes of Pat Quinn and Gary Doak."

The WHA even made overtures to Kurtenbach, but that

old Vancouver connection was too strong to sever, and he decided to play out his career with the Canucks, retiring in the spring of 1974 after 639 regular season NHL games.

Kurtenbach's playing days might have been over in the mid 1970s, but his association with West Coast hockey was far from complete. A Centennial Cup Championship would come to Kurtenbach as the coach of the Richmond Sockeyes in 1987, defeating the host Humboldt Broncos in the final.

Now his coaching days are also behind Kurtenbach, but his dedication to the game remains steel-strong as he works in marketing and community relations with the British Columbia Hockey League. Among his accomplishments for the BCHL is to have the Canuck Alumni—whom he still plays for in fundraising games—provide scholarships for B.C. players in the league to attend university in the province. To date, that has lead to $135,000 in support of BCHL players from the alumni group.

Kurtenbach also remains a strong advocate of Tier II Junior "A", seeing some dollars flowing from the NHL for players who go through the 138 teams across the country to be drafted. As it stands, the level has about the same number of draftees annually as United States colleges or players from Europe, he said. "We've been asking for funding for players that get drafted," he said, suggesting a figure of $600,000 has been discussed, but to no avail as of yet.

For Kurtenbach, it's all part of giving back to a sport he loves, in a part of Canada he now proudly calls home. It's an effort that has not gone unnoticed. He was the 1986 winner of the Jake Milford Plaque for outstanding service to hockey in B.C., and has been elected to the B.C. Hockey Hall of Fame.

Keep Your Travel Bags Packed

Brent Ashton had a National Hockey League career which spanned 14 years, and played just two regular season games short of 1,000. Given the longevity the Saskatoon-born Ashton had at the premier level of the sport, you might expect he was a long-time veteran toiling for years for the same team, which grew to appreciate his gritty, hardworking style. But that was not the case.

Instead, Ashton became something of a hired gun, one who kept his travel bags packed in readiness for yet another trade. Over his career, Ashton would lace up his skates and don the sweater of nine different NHL franchises. It wasn't the career he initially envisioned, but it evolved that way, and he took it in stride.

"The first one was the hardest [moving from Vancouver, the team that drafted him 26th overall in 1979, to Colorado]. You go thinking you're going to be there for a long time," he said.

As it was, Ashton looks at his rookie season as an accomplishment, being one of only three 18-year-olds to stick with their team through the entire season, playing 47 games and having 19 points. But when the deals started, and Ashton found himself regularly on the move, he said he learned to deal with it in the most positive manner possible.

"It was an adjustment to every team you went to," he said, noting that he tried to play the role needed, playing all three forward positions, and assuming both offensive and defensive roles throughout his career. "On one team you might be fourth line and go somewhere else and you couldn't get off the ice."

Ashton said it was a case of just staying focused on hockey. "It was just playing with that level of confidence," he said. The confidence level was maintained by recognizing a team only trades for someone they expect can help improve their roster. "You start to realize you're going to a team that wants you. That's the way you have to look at it. You're filling a need that they have."

Even with a good outlook on trades, at times they came as a surprise. Such was the case when, part way through 1987–88, Ashton found himself on the move from Detroit to the Winnipeg Jets. "Detroit was kind of a shock," he said. "I was coming off a 40-goal year between them [the Red Wings] and Quebec."

The 40-goal season remains the one Ashton looks at as his best in the NHL. "I had some other good years, but that year... was special."

So too was his time as a member of the long-gone Nordiques in Quebec City. Ashton said particular goals from his long career just don't stick out at all. Asked about his first NHL goal, he knows it was when he was with Vancouver, but no particulars. "I can't remember that far back. It was in Vancouver. I was just an 18-year-old kid," he said. Nor does the last goal of his career register as a memory. "It was just a blur. I don't remember that goal either."

But there were nights in Quebec that have stuck, even if the exact dates haven't. "I had six points one night, three goals and three assists. That was special. I remember all the press, and holding up the two pucks for photographs," he said. In Quebec, Ashton remembers a game seven overtime win against Montreal at the fabled forum too."It was quite a rivalry back then," he said.

Ashton expected more memories in Quebec, until the trade came. That was at the time the Wings were overloaded at left wing, and thin at right wing because Bob Probert was having difficulty crossing the Canada/United States border."So one of the left wingers had to go to bring in a right winger," he said. Since he was coming off a 40-goal season,"that's when you're stock is the highest."

Leaving Detroit was harder because it was a great place to play."Mr. [Mike] Ilitch was great to the players, and playing in front of 20,000 fans every night was great," he said. He went to the Stanley Cup semi-finals in both 1987 and 1988 with the Wings.

At the same time, Ashton couldn't choose a favourite team from among the nine he played with—he had stops in Vancouver, Colorado, New Jersey, Minnesota, Quebec, Detroit, Winnipeg, Boston and Calgary."I think each city had something very positive about it," he said. For example, Boston was great as an original-six franchise and Winnipeg"was a very close team." He had a career-high 31 goals with the Jets in 1988–89, the same year he won a silver medal playing for Canada at the World Championships.

Being on the move as often as Ashton was also afforded him a rare opportunity to play alongside many of his era's best players. He lined up with the likes of Steve Yzerman in Detroit, Peter and Anton Stastny in Quebec, and Ray Bourque in Boston.

Ashton looks back on his career in the NHL with no regrets about how he played the game. He had 284 goals, and added 345 assists for 629 points. Of course, he wished he had a Stanley Cup ring to cherish—he made the semi finals three times."That's why every kid plays the game. They want to score the goal to win that

Cup or be on the team to hoist that Cup," he said. "But a lot of great players never get to do that."

As it was, Ashton realized his dream just to play in the NHL. As a youth he was the typical Saskatchewan rink rat. "Back then it was more school hockey. All the schools kind of had rinks and you played outdoors, so that's where the competition kind of came from," he said. "You played an hour before school started. You played at recess, at noon hour and after school until it was time to go for supper."

If that wasn't enough to set Ashton on a path to the NHL, by the time he was 13, he was stick boy for the Western Hockey League Saskatoon Blades where his older brother Ron played. "It was great being able to practice and skate with them two or three times a week. I'd take the bus downtown for practices after school. That was a big part of my development at a young age, watching and playing with the older guys."

Ashton was obviously a quick study. While he played one AAA Midget game against a touring Russian team with the Saskatoon Blazers—a team his father Ken helped launch—he was playing with the Blades at 15.

As a 15-year-old in the WHL, Ashton said there was an adjustment to the speed and size of the game at the level, but he never shied away from the flow of the game. "Watching as a stick boy all those years, I guess I knew what to expect," he said.

In his final season as a Blade, 1978–79, Ashton had a standout year with 64 goals and 55 assists for 119 points. His four seasons with Saskatoon, and his NHL career, were marked by the WHL team in November 2004, when his #7 jersey was retired. It was just the fourth in franchise history, following those of Wendel Clark, Bernie Federko and Brian Skrudland.

"I was very honoured to know every time we go to the arena from now on it will always be there," he said. "It was a special evening for me and my family, especially for my parents. They're the ones that made the big sacrifice."

While the ceremony did bring back memories of his junior days as a Blade, Ashton said, "I never really played in that rink. I played in the old one, so there were no memories that way."

Playing junior in his home town was a big plus. "I was very lucky to be able to live at home and play junior hockey, so I still had that parental guidance," he said. "I have a lot of respect for those kids making that commitment to move away and live with billets for their hockey."

When it came time for Ashton's draft year, he thought he was heading to Winnipeg. "They had called lots and talked to me about coming down and signing a contract," he said. But the Jets took Jimmy Mann, and Ashton was heading to the Canucks in Vancouver. In the end, he didn't care which team took him. "Back then you just wanted to play, it didn't matter who for or for how much.

"When I went there [Vancouver] they asked 'what number do you want?' I said it didn't matter, I just wanted a jersey on my back."

For Ashton, the game has come full circle. He's back in Saskatoon working with his wife Susan's sport clothing business, and coaching the game, including his son Carter's Bantam team, and working with the SaskFirst program. "I'm trying to give something back to the kids," he said. One day he would like to become involved behind the bench at the junior level as well.

As for his sons, Carter is the hockey player, while Taylor has moved on to snowboarding. Ashton simply tries to encourage their passions. "As a father you just want to give direction. If it's something they enjoy doing, you give them every opportunity to do it, whether it's snowboarding or hockey," he said.

Whether it's Ashton's own sons or the kids he coaches, they can learn from the former NHLer's dedication to the game, which he played with heart, grit and enough skill around the net to keep him in the big show for nearly a decade and a half—he had seven 20-goal seasons. "I had to work that much harder than a lot of guys to stay up there. I trained hard in summer. I did a lot extra to play at that level," he said. "It's just how good do you want to get. That's what it comes down to."

Ashton said he appreciated when people recognized the effort he put into being successful at the game. "When fans came up and said they really enjoyed watching you play and that 'you worked hard', that was great. If people paying money to watch you play enjoyed the effort you put forward, that's very rewarding."

Woman in the Striped Shirt

In the world of hockey, the women's side of the game has been growing by leaps and bounds. Much of the success in the female ranks is because there were pioneers who persevered and opened doors for those who would follow.

In Sarina Baker's case, the opportunity to play a game she loved from the stands never presented itself, but that didn't stop her from forging a place for herself in the game. Instead of finding her way on to hockey teams in her hometown of Glenavon, she donned the striped shirt of an official. "It was pretty much because my parents didn't let me play hockey," she said with a laugh.

There was a lure to the game Baker couldn't escape. "I loved the intensity, the fast skating, the hard hitting. It's all about intensity..."

It was also a part of Saskatchewan culture Baker felt was a natural to follow, whether male or female. "You were always at the rink. You took every opportunity to be on the ice every second you could be," she said, adding that growing up on the farm she always looked forward "to going into town to go skating...So I talked to my dad and told him I wanted to go to a clinic to be a referee."

Where her parents barred the door to playing the game, they opened the door for Baker to become an official. At 14, she took the clinic, and two weeks later was in a game as a linesman.

The local Pee Wee coach was the first to call one night when he was responsible for finding a linesman for a game. Baker said there was pressure to be good in her role right from the start, but all young officials felt it in those days. "If you weren't working very hard or you weren't very good, you wouldn't get called back. There was always somebody else wanting the games."

Baker said two coaches gave her the opportunity to grow into her chosen role: Norman McKay and Joey Stajniak. She owed them a big thank you. It helped her brother was a player, and often she'd get to lines on road games "because my parents were already going anyway."

Still, it may have eased her transition into a role where females were rarely seen in the late 1980s. "In rural Saskatchewan, they were just happy to have somebody available to do games," she said.

That being said, there were those who suggested hockey was no place for a girl, even if she was wearing stripes. Often the suggestion was that figure skating was the better place for her. Baker laughs at that now. "I actually was a figure skater at the same time. I would figure skate until seven, and do a change and go back on the ice as a referee."

Initially, Baker said no one was exactly pleased to see her on the ice as an official. "From the fans I was getting 'what's a girl doing out there? You're going to get hurt or killed out there'," said Baker. "...The coaches and players came around quickly after dealing with me on the ice...The hardest people to get to accept me was the fans."

From the players it was more distrust. "[What] do you know about hockey? You're just a girl," recalled Baker. She worked hard to be prepared. "I made sure my rule knowledge was high, so that I almost always knew the answer without hesitation." Even then it was never easy in the beginning. "No matter if you were equal, you had to work twice as hard."

There were also the inevitable problems of women moving into a male world where facilities were designed for men only. "As a female official, we didn't get our own dressing room. The SHA protocol is that the gender of official that is the minority changes last. We take turns sharing the room. It took some time to get the message across, so it was my responsibility to plan ahead. I would, and still do, get to the arena before the other officials and get changed before everyone else. This way I had adequate time to get dressed and mentally prepared."

Baker said she never let the naysayers get to her for long, and she credits her parents for that. "I knew there was nothing I couldn't do. My parents instilled that in me...My parents were my support system," she said.

Support system or not, Baker got her opportunity and immediately knew she had found her place in the game. "I just felt incredible out on the ice. I was scared to death, but totally invigorated by it too," she said. "For me it was the light bulb that turned on, and I knew it's where I wanted to be," she said, adding the feeling has never left her. "The tingling in the toes and the excitement in the heart said it was where I needed to be. I still feel it every time I step on the ice."

That isn't to suggest there weren't moments of doubt for the young official. "The only time I can remember seriously thinking about quitting was early in my career. It was during the middle of provincials and league playoffs and I was taken as the away linesman to a Midget playoff game in Kipling. It was my responsibility to notify the referee that one of the players from my hometown, their top defenceman, had speared another player behind the play.

"I didn't hesitate.

"The player ended up getting suspended during the middle of playoffs and needless to say my hometown didn't support me. I was no longer asked to officiate any local games. The only reason I didn't quit was a neighbouring town, Kipling, continued to call me.

"If it wasn't for this, I think it would have been devastating to my career—Heaven forbid, things could have ended up very differently."

For Baker, her real break into the officials' ranks came in 1997, when she went to the Western Canadian Shield Women's Championship in Edmonton. "I ended up doing the gold medal final based on merit," she said. "I thought I was going to be a professional linesman. It all came down to confidence and the Western Canadian Shield in Edmonton opened my door...I'd always had the bug of officiating, but the referee bug of being the boss has been since then. From that you can come home and pretty well accomplish anything."

To Baker's knowledge, she became the first woman in Saskatchewan to achieve her Level 4 as an official, meaning she is qualified to do international games, including World Championships. With such credentials, Baker has officiated across Canada, including several National Championships and the Canada Winter Games. She recalled her first one, and the feeling of being at centre ice with Hayley Wickenheiser involved. "My first National Championship, I was dropping the puck and she [Wickenheiser] wouldn't put her stick down. I got to throw her out of the faceoff circle. There was a tingle in my toes realizing who it was."

For Baker, a Canada Games match sticks out most in her

mind. "The most memorable game for me was the Bronze Medal Final at the Canada Winter Games in 1999. I was told by the evaluators from the tournament that two of us officials were neck and neck for the gold medal game. They decided to give me the bronze game based on my home province was in the game, and I had the mental toughness to get through the challenge. Whoever thought that ending up third was more honouring than second? The game ended up going into triple overtime with Saskatchewan losing. It was the longest, most rewarding game of my life."

The number of big games Baker has been involved in illustrates the opportunities that exist for young female officials, she said. "In women's hockey you have so much potential to do so many great things in such a short period of time," she said.

Still, there remain times being an official makes Baker wonder about her role on the ice. "I have never felt that I have lost control of a game, but I have felt like I lost control of my composure and emotions. This happened this season. After 16 years of officiating, I let the pressure of duelling coaches get to me. It didn't matter what I did that game, nobody seemed to be happy, and didn't seem to take the message that penalties were going to continue being called.

"To finalize the message I got angry and loud and filled the penalty box, until the message was understood.

"After talking to others it was found that I perceived my actions to be worse than the perception from the other officials, coaches and fans. It was that moment that I began to seek guidance on mental toughness training. It was the beginning of a strong season for me."

Baker took on the role of Developmental Coordinator for Female Officials with the Saskatchewan Hockey Association in 2000, and at the time there were only 88 female officials in the province. Five years later, in 2005, the number has doubled to 175, but even then the numbers are so low, opportunities to advance quickly remain. As an example, there are some 3,500 male officials in the province, all with a desire to go to the national level. On the women's side, choices are made from among the 175.

Now in charge of the development of young female officials, Baker said she is finding it as rewarding as blowing the whistle herself. "It's not just about me. I get as much satisfaction out of seeing young officials develop...It's so gratifying to have been a part of the support group helping them succeed...

"I've been very lucky I've had the support to succeed, and it's great seeing everybody else have the opportunity to succeed."

With young female officials emerging, Baker has pulled herself off the list to do the national tournaments. "There are more young officials of similar qualifications that deserve an opportunity," she said.

In Saskatchewan though, the opportunity to officiate women's games are limited. Baker does do university women's games, and the new Saskatchewan Prairie Ice team in the Western Women's Hockey League provides another opportunity.

"But I do mostly men's games. I do a lot of senior hockey," she said, adding it took a while for a 5-foot-5, 125 pound official to find favour with competitive senior players. "They'd come up and make a couple of comments, and you just stand your ground and show them you're not afraid," she said. "Your job is to just let them play."

Now content to ref senior games—Baker said she enjoys working in the Wheatland, Fort Carlton and Sask Valley hockey leagues, something she does for herself, and the love of the game—she looks back and recognizes there were bumps in the road to her success as an official, but there are no regrets. "None at all. No matter how bad things got I basically learned something from it. It's all paid off. Every day that was a challenge has helped make me who I am...Now I just want others to see the joys it [being an official] brings."

Baker said she's proud to be involved in women's hockey, adding the growth of hockey on the female side has "been tremendous. When I started it was in its infancy [compared] to what it is now, and it's still probably only in its adolescence. It still has so far to go."

From her perspective, Baker only sees growth, adding as women gain foot speed and hand skills, with better, more focused training, the game will evolve into a European-style hockey. "I see an international league in 10 years. I look at the 13-year-olds, and how seriously they take the game, the way they model themselves on Team Canada. Imagine them at 18."

Pair Has Major Success with Minor Career

When you look into the record book of the now defunct International Hockey League, and in particular the records of the Muskegon/Cleveland Lumberjacks, two Saskatchewan players figure prominently. Jock Callander and Dave Michayluk were teammates for years in the Lumberjack organization and racked up tons of points as line mates. However, the duo actually came together in Regina when both played for the Western Hockey League Pats.

Michayluk said the pair may have faced off against each other in Midget without really recognizing it, but once they were matched as linemates in 1981, something special occurred. "Sometimes it's like magic. The two of us just read off each other so well," he said. That season Michayluk had 178 points, while Callander had 190. That was outstanding success for two players who didn't immediately start their junior careers at the WHL level.

As Callander neared junior age, he decided to head to Providence College, but he didn't get the ice time or success he had hoped for, and when Bob Strumm with the Regina Pats of the Western Hockey League came calling, the young forward was listening.

The Pats at the time were deep in talent with the likes of Doug Wickenheiser and Ron Flockhart. "These guys were tearing it up that season, so I came back at Christmas time."

The decision proved a good one, as the Pats headed to the Memorial Cup in Callander's first year of 1979. "It was fun," he said, although he wasn't a huge contributor to the Pats, who lost out to Cornwall.

Two seasons later the scorer Callander blossomed. At 17, he had a goal-a-game season with the Pat Canadians, and in his third year in the WHL he had 67 goals and 153 points in 72 games. A season later he upped that production to 79 goals and 190 points.

"I was always good around the net, so I got some points," he said with a laugh. Throughout his career the power play was where he often seemed most at home scoring goals. "They were a big chunk of my stats. I seemed to get a lot of my points on the power play."

He got a big chunk of his points with Michayluk too. The two would go on to be linemates for years, extending beyond Junior to their years in the pros, but the pair met under less than ideal circumstances. "The year I came back from college, we went on a West Coast trip and lost our last game in New Westminster, and they weren't that good a team that season," recalled Callander. So the Pats coach called up a couple of rookies for the next game. One was Michayluk, who played as Callander enjoyed a night sitting in the stands watching.

Both players had what are typical hockey starts for boys from Saskatchewan, although Michayluk would also take a different route to the Pats. "I started in Wakaw when I was six years old. A cousin of mine got me interested in it. He was a year older and just starting too," said Michayluk. For Michayluk to play though, a commitment had to be made by his parents. Living on a farm 10 miles from town meant he couldn't just grab his gear and walk to the local rink. "They made themselves a real commitment. With games and practices it was into town two or three times a week, and my younger brother played too, and we weren't on the same teams. It was almost everyday [travel] sometimes."

Michayluk would learn more about life on the winter road in Saskatchewan when he played with a Junior "B" team in Prince Albert at the age of 16. The team was a farm club of the Prince Albert Raiders, then of the Saskatchewan Junior Hockey League, and the young skater lived at home and drove the 50 miles in for practices and games all winter.

The driving paid off come springtime when he was called up to the Raiders, who were hosting the Centennial Cup tournament to crown the best junior team at that level. "We won the Centennial Cup that year [spring of 1979]," said Michayluk. "I played some through the playoffs for them, and then in the tournament."

It was a quick taste of success at a high level, which Michayluk liked. "I guess it's always exciting when you win," he said with a chuckle. "It was pretty exciting."

Obviously Michayluk impressed the Raiders, as he stayed with the team the following season, where he came under the wing of PA coach Terry Simpson. "He was good. I still meet him and talk. He had something about him. He could get the best out of guys...He had a knack."

The year with the Raiders was important for Michayluk, who got plenty of ice. Looking back, he knows he made the right choice in staying in PA that season, even though the Regina Pats had wanted him there. He said the level of talent on the Pats was such he would have spent too much time sitting to have improved.

However, after one season in PA, he did make the move south to the Queen city. He said the decision came rather easily, even though he was leaving a powerhouse franchise in the Raiders. "When I was growing up, I said I want to make the Raiders and I did that, so this was another step," he said. "I decided I wanted to go farther, and that was the logical choice."

At the time, Michayluk said the step to the Pats was not a large one after playing with the Raiders. "Back then when I did it, it wasn't that big a step. The Raiders were such a good team, maybe that helped," he said.

Callander's hockey started and stayed in his hometown through junior. "It was just basically going to the outdoor rink. Sherwood School was just a couple of blocks way. Dad used to take me there," said Callander of his earliest hockey memories.

Callander's father Len was a long-time minor hockey coach, focusing on the 15 to 16 age group, meaning he didn't simply follow his son through the levels. "My dad has always loved hockey."

Callander said in his days it was the norm for school kids just to pick teams and play. He wishes today, "kids could get some more of that energy for the game." Instead, today's minor hockey seems too pressure packed, with kids expected to excel at an early age.

Callander talks about a youth where he admits he was not the most talented player. "I never played organized hockey until I was about eight and that was only a few games of Tom Thumb. We weren't really organized in a league. I was nine years old when I really got started."

Before that, and even through the minor hockey to come, Callander said he and brother Drew were always playing the game. "It was always hockey. We played in the streets, we played on the outdoor rinks," he said. That was about all there was to do. "We didn't have computers and video games."

"I think something has changed. There's so much more to do. Our outdoor rink was played on all the time."

Kids used to learn some of the finesse and magic of the game during that time on the outdoor rinks, Callander said. "Today kids can skate and shoot, but they don't have the imagination players used to have. They're all robotic now. They look like clones out there.

"You used to see some unbelievable players. Now it's all dump it in and chase.

"It was the outdoor rinks where kids learned the creativity and imagination."

While Callander loved the game, the skills that would blossom into a near 20-year pro career didn't manifest themselves at a young age. "I was probably an average to below average player," he said. "I wasn't a very good skater." In fact, his first Bantam AA tryout ended with him being cut from the team, moving him from the Pat Canadiens team to the Silver Foxes that year. The Silver Foxes were in their last year in the North Saskatchewan League, and were not a powerhouse, but it was a chance for Callander to play.

In his second year at the level, Callander said "I had a pretty good year, and that got me thinking about better things." As Callander moved up through the minor system to the junior ranks, he developed, especially as a goal scorer. "I was kind of a late bloomer when I was young. A lot of kids were better than me. I pretty well had to work to keep up with everybody."

While the pair would put up impressive numbers when teamed on the Pats, Callander was not drafted out of the Junior ranks. Michayluk was taken in the draft by Philadelphia, going in the fourth round, 65th overall in 1981.

"I signed as a free agent with St. Louis," said Callander. He was assigned to Salt Lake City in the Central Hockey League his first pro season.

Looking back, Callander's start in the pros, coming off such high production seasons in Regina, was a difficult time. "That was frustrating. In Salt Lake City I didn't play hardly at all. I sat in the stands a lot of games. That was the way it was back then. You had to earn your chance. Vets played no matter what...Now when you get drafted you're given all kinds of chances."

Sitting on the sidelines and not getting a real break through two years in the minors did not sit well with Callander, who said he was contemplating leaving pro hockey and returning to university in Regina. Then along came Rick Ley with Muskegon of the old International Hockey League. "He sort of revived my career. He was a very good coach and he renewed my confidence."

One of the differences as a Lumberjack under Ley was that Callander was once more allowed to focus more attention on offence, and the numbers soon returned. His first two seasons in Muskegon Callander scored 39 goals each year. Callander also tasted success right off the bat, as his first season with the Lumberjacks saw the team go all the way to the Turner Cup finals before losing.

In 1985, Callander and Michayluk would also be reunited as Lumberjack teammates, and the magic remained. "It went on for years and years. It never seemed to change," said Michayluk, who added the two had rare careers, being together so long. "It never happens now. It's money and trades and guys end up going all over the place."

The move to the Lumberjacks also helped Callander get another shot at the NHL, signing with Pittsburgh. His first camp he was among the Penguins' first cuts, something he blames on working out too much over the summer. Back in Muskegon, though, he said, "I went on a tear right off the start."

The start would get Callander a call-up to Pittsburgh, where he played 41 games his first season. Initially he was scoring at pretty much a point-a-game clip, but then his ice time diminished, something he took in stride. "I was just enjoying the time up there. That was the place I always wanted to be."

Callander said as an offensive forward, the Penguins were a tough team to crack, with the likes of Mario Lemieux, March Recchi and Ron Francis on the team.

So during his time under a Pittsburgh contract, Callander bounced back and forth to Muskegon. The most interesting bounce came in 1992. He would not play a regular season NHL game that year, but was called up for the Pens' playoff run after Lemieux was hurt while facing the New York Rangers. "I played the rest of the games in that series."

Right there with Callander for the playoff call-up was Michayluk, who played in seven games as well. "It was just the experience of being there with the players and seeing and feeling the atmosphere," he said. "So many guys never get a chance. We were fortunate just to be there."

Being there together added to the sweetness for Michayluk. "It made it a little extra special. We had gone through a lot together, all the bumps and bus rides and late nights."

Callander would dress the rest of the way, although ice time diminished as injured players returned. He would get into 12 playoff games that season, ending up with his name on the Stanley Cup. "It was still the most amazing time. They made me feel part of the team," he said. "When you think about players like Marcel Dionne and Gilbert Perreault who never won a Stanley Cup, you feel very fortunate to have been there."

Following the Stanley Cup win, Callander was on his way to the expansion Tampa Bay Lightning in search of greater NHL ice time. The last day before the season started, he was back in the minors. "Before Christmas I was back and forth a lot, but I only played in eight games [for Tampa]." He was offered a termination contract, and opted to instead return to the IHL with the Lumberjacks, who were by 1993 in Cleveland. "That was when the "I" was offering some bigger contracts," he said. He went for the money and the Lumberjacks "were a good fit."

Callander said he has no regrets playing 17 years of pro hockey, even if that includes only 109 regular season NHL games. "I wish I would have had a few more games just to see what I could have done. It would have been nice to not be on the fourth line getting maybe two shifts a period," he said. Then he added, "But, I still had a good career."

Good indeed, setting the IHL's all-time leading scorer mark with 1,402 IHL career points on 554 goals, and 848 assists. "If I had it all to do over again I'd play another 18 years in the minors. I met a ton of great people."

Michayluk played fewer NHL games, only 14 regular season contests with the Flyers during his rookie campaign. Still, he believes he and Callander just needed a better chance. "You always think that. Part of it is timing, being in the right place at the right time," he said, admitting being in the Penguins system at the height of that team's success didn't help. "I still think if we'd been given a real good shot, I think we could have played there [NHL]."

In fact, Michayluk said with the attitude today, he'd probably have done things differently in that first season with the Flyers. He said he was off to a good start, with eight points in 13 games, but at 20 was sent down, as a 32-year-old was kept in Philly. "I would have done things a little differently if I was doing it now...I'd say, 'No, I proved I can play here. I deserve to be here'. Guys are doing that now."

At the time, players simply followed orders. "Whatever they told you, you shook your head and did it. You didn't argue. You didn't get the agents involved."

That being said, Michayluk doesn't regret playing. "I loved the game. We got treated good by owner Larry Gordon... We did our own contracts. We sat down and haggled it out... We could argue over a contract and then walk down the street, and have a beer with him."

That relationship bred loyalty, something Michayluk said you see less and less of in hockey. "Loyalty now is whoever gives the bigger bucks, you're gone."

Still, Michayluk can look back on a junior Centennial Cup, three Turner Cups in the IHL, and a Stanley Cup. "I'd have loved to spend my career in the NHL. It just didn't work out, but I had a great career in the minors." His career in the IHL covered 968 regular season games, 547 goals, 636 assists for 1,183 points.

Still, Michayluk hung them up ahead of Callander, retiring to the family farm at Wakaw after the 1996–97 season. "It was easy for me. I just knew. I had reached a point in my career, I wasn't happy anymore. It got to the point I wasn't happy going to the rink, so it was time."

Now he farms as his father did, while continuing to play recreational hockey for fun and driving his three daughters Madison, Kortney and Lauren to games."

He and Callander remain friends, a relationship forged through years of hockey. "We did everything together. We roomed together on the road. We ate together. We walked to the rink in the morning together," said Callander.

The Art of the Mask

Goaltenders are often viewed as just a little different from their hockey brethren. Adding to their aura of individuality is the way many netminders have the masks they wear when guarding the twine custom painted. Incorporating the personality of the goaltender into the art falls to a small group of artists dedicated to capturing the mood of team and netminder on an unusual canvas of fiberglass.

For Art Lima, the idea of creating goalie mask art was a true natural, given his artistic interest and his involvement in the game. "I'm a goalie for starters. I've painted masks really since I was a kid. I remember taking ball hockey masks, taping them up and painting them using aerosol cans [of paint]." Much more recently, Lima took up airbrush painting, and goaltender masks were a natural support to start working with. He said the support was a good one to learn airbrushing on, and he has nearly 100 masks to his credit now. "It's mostly parents buying them, or their kids it seems," said Lima.

Even in junior hockey, creative masks have become familiar sights as witnessed in the Saskatchewan Junior Hockey League. B.J. Skalapsky played with the Humboldt Broncos in the 2002–03 season, and was among the top-rated netminders in the SJHL, as well as sporting one of the most unique masks. He said the masks goaltenders wear add a flavour to the game. "I think it adds a little bit more fun to the game," said Skalapsky. "You see guys with painted cages and you want to see what's on their masks."

Skalapsky's mask included visages of two Grim Reapers as well as the words "Fear the Keeper." The mask was custom painted by John Chubak of Saskatoon. "Basically I gave him an idea of what I wanted and he went to work," said Skalapsky, who has kept the same theme through three incarnations dating back to his days in Bantam hockey. "The Grim Reaper idea has stuck with me the whole time," he said.

An airbrush artist, Chubak said his involvement in painting masks came almost by accident. Chubak had always liked to draw, but found his artistic niche when his wife gave him an airbrush in 1996. "I just put my heart into it. It was something I thought I could be good at," he said.

Since then, his "canvases" read a little like a list of articles at a corner yard sale. He said he has painted toilet seats (adding with a chuckle that he only paints new ones), cell phones, bowling pins, guitars, snowboards, Harley Davidsons, Hummers, and yes, goalie masks.

"A guy at work wanted me to do his goalie mask, and after that it was word-of-mouth, one would come, and then another," he said. He is probably nearing 200 he has painted over the last few years.

Chubak enjoys doing the masks, knowing they'll be viewed by hundreds of fans.

"They're a smaller item too," he said. "I can handle it. I can turn it around easier to work on."

Ideally, a goaltender provides a basic idea and then allows Chubak the artistic freedom to be creative around the chosen theme. "Those are the best ones, who let me have a free rein on the work. They say 'I have an idea, here, go with it'," he said.

Lima agreed the best works often emerge with artistic freedom. "A lot of times they show you their team logo and let you design something for it. When you can create on your own, that's where you get your best work."

On the other end of the scale is the perfectionist who has every detail of a mask visualized and wants it done exactly to his vision. Chubak recalled a visiting Neil Diamond impersonator from Las Vegas who was also a goaltender. The mask design included numerous elements like the Statue of Liberty, flared playing cards and a standing goaltender. "He was on tour across the country and I'd get a call from a different city every couple of nights," said Chubak, who paints under the name Venomous Air.

Of course there are limits to Chubak's comfort zone with the ideas goaltenders envision. "I have my limits of what I'll put on a mask," he said. "One guy wanted a referee crucified on a cross. I didn't think that was appropriate."

Lima admits to a darker side. He is an ITECH-certified mask painter—meaning he has submitted a detailed listing of his process of disassembling, painting and putting a mask back together, which has been approved by the manufacturer. As a follow-up to the process, ITECH supplied a couple of goaltender mask blanks for Lima to paint and return for an up-close inspection of his work. "One of them was fairly wild. It was all different skulls and flames," he said. His other passion is motorcycles, and he airbrushes a lot of gas tanks.

Still, in the end the work is often stunning, and as an artist Chubak said it can be difficult to see a mask leave the shop knowing it will be abused on the ice every night, and most likely painted over in time. He has goaltenders who have new art applied every season or two. "I've done some jobs that it was very hard to give back. I thought 'wow, to me these look really nice'."

Since a goaltender mask is destined for the abuse of frozen rubber propelled at slapshot speed, Lima said he uses paints from the auto industry to ensure they stand up to the abuse.

Todd Veary, a goaltender with the Yorkton Terriers in 2002–03, tried to infuse his mask with both the team and himself in mind. "I did the orange because I knew there was orange on the Terriers," he said. For the main focus of the mask Veary turned to the movie character "Jason," more specifically from his most recent film where the horror icon awakens in the future.

"Jason evolves into a more futuristic guy," said Veary. With the change, the goalie-mask-wearing psycho donned a more futuristic mask too. "That's why I wanted to make mine more futuristic too. Most goalies will do a paint job that fits their personality or the team they play on," he said. "I just wanted something kind of different a bit....Something you haven't seen done on a mask."

With the basic idea in mind, Veary handed the mask to Quebec artist Stephen Bergeron to create the finished product, adding he was eager to see the result. "When you tell him [the artist] to let his imagination go, that's when you're most anxious," he said. "But when I went and got it, I was just thrilled by the way it came out."

Veary said looking to the Jason character for inspiration really had him returning to his younger years. "It was the first horror movie that I saw as a kid," he said. He was fascinated by the idea of Jason wearing a goaltender's mask. The more futuristic look that fits his team by colour and his interest in the movie is a nice combination.

Veary's father has kept the Yorkton netminder's first five painted masks. "It's just the thing that it's a memory," said Veary of his father's growing collection. His first painted mask goes back to Novice. The Novice mask was repeatedly re-painted as he changed teams, starting off as a copy of former NHL netminder Kirk McLean's mask, and ending up sort of like the comic character The Shadow when he played summer hockey on a team called the Bandits.

Jamie Langen faced off against the likes of Veary and Skalapsky as he toiled with the Melville Millionaires. Langen ended up with a mask very reflective of the team he plays on. Representing the Millionaires concept, Langen's mask has Scrooge McDuck on one side and the Monopoly character on the other. "I just kind of wanted something that represented the Millionaires," he said, adding the idea evolved. "My first idea was Bob Barker and The Price Is Right. That led me to do Scrooge McDuck. The ideas just kinda came from teammates."

The mask is the first in Langen's career to be something other than standard black or white, a rarity among today's netminders. "I didn't really think it was a priority to me to have my helmet painted," he said, although he admitted he is already thinking of more detailed ideas for his next paint job.

For his first mask Langen turned to local Yorkton artist Damian Shishkin to create the final product. Shishkin, 25, said he has found a passion for painting masks. "I've been into art all my life. This is the best way I've found to express it," he said. "...I've been doing it since high school. It started with a couple of floor hockey masks."

Since then the work has included not only Langen's mask, but that of a visiting goaltender from Australia, junior hockey netminders and a mask for Yorkton lacrosse keeper Cory Exner. "It's relaxing. It gives me a break from everything else," he said.

Preferably, Shishkin would be making a career of painting masks, but it's rather seasonal work. "Once hockey season starts they don't want to be without their masks for a month," he said.

Lima said ideally, goaltenders should think ahead and have their masks painted in the off-season, but that is not the reality. Most want their masks done as the season starts in the fall, with another flush at Christmas as gifts. Often the gift is done as a surprise, but Lima said that may not be the best plan. "It's better to have input from the goalie. They usually have a pretty good idea of what they want."

The process of painting a mask takes time. Lima estimated a month for his busy schedule, while Shishkin said his painting method took about two weeks, once he and the client have agreed on sketched designs.

Working closely on the design is a must, said Shishkin, since masks are such a personal item to netminders. "It's a personal thing. They want something that expresses themselves," he said. The trend is to ignore team concepts in favour of something personal. "Take Ed Belfour in the NHL. He's had the same mask design all along, he just changes it to team colours," said Shishkin.

Once a mask is painted, it takes another two weeks to clear coat it properly. "It takes two weeks to get it sealed, so if a puck hits it, it doesn't chip," he said.

Sean Connors of the Kindersley Klippers decided to don his current painted helmet when the team he was with last season offered to have it done for him. "Last year they offered to get it painted, and I thought I might as well go along with it," he said.

The idea for Connors' mask came from bouncing ideas around the dressing room. "I threw out my ideas and guys just kind of threw ideas back," he said. "One of the guys on the team gave me the idea of the girls on the side."

Getting a newly painted helmet is a big moment for a goaltender, seeing their ideas for the first time as a piece of completed sports art. "Everybody was pretty excited to see the outcome," recalled Connors, who at the time was in Medicine Hat of the Western Hockey League, where the local newspaper even did a story on the new mask.

"And I was quite excited. I had seen it a couple of times just in pencil, but seeing it finished was great."

Like Skalapsky, Connors has been wearing painted creations since Bantam hockey. As he has progressed, the art has focused more on the team he is playing with. The first two masks now sit in Connors' basement as memory markers of his hockey career to date. "The two for the Western League were definitely focused on what the team was all about," he said, adding they must have an element of "self" as well.

"I still think the biggest part is for it [the art] to come from yourself, and just fit that in with the team itself."

European Route to World Championships

Jamie Heward may not have played 250 games in the National Hockey League, but he does have two World Championship gold medals. Heward said he felt nervous, being the only player on the Team Canada roster at both Championships—2003 in Finland and 2004 in Czechoslovakia—who was not at the time in the NHL. He felt he belonged on the roster, though.

"I had played a lot more NHL games than a lot of guys on the team," he said. "In retrospect I think I was just as qualified as everybody else."

That being said, looking around the dressing room Heward realized what good company he was keeping. "To be there in the mix was just an unbelievable feeling," he said.

Heward said the importance of the gold medal surprised him too. "All these things are coming at you from all over. You don't appreciate how big it is.

"Everybody in Canada would love to put on the Canadian jersey and play an international game."

The opportunity to play wearing the Canadian jersey is one of the big pluses of playing in Europe, said Heward, who headed to Switzerland to play after the 1999–00 season. "The great thing about playing over here is getting to play in four or five international tournaments with Team Canada," he said.

For Heward, a defenceman on the ice, that has meant play in such tournaments as the Spengler Cup, Lotto Cup and Deutschland Cup. "That in itself is awesome," he said. "You put on the jersey, whether it's the World Championships, the Olympics of the Spengler Cup, you're still representing Canada, and everybody wants to beat you."

Heward said events such as the Spengler Cup are only now getting some recognition in Canada because of expanded cable television coverage, but the games have always meant something to players. They may not be as high profile as Joe Thornton and Martin St. Louis, who also play for Canada, "But we still play for our country just as hard as they do."

Playing in the lesser known international events opened the door to something bigger for Heward when he received the call to try out for Team Canada for the 2003 World Championships in Finland. "I couldn't believe it, three or four guys had turned it down," said Heward, who eagerly accepted the invitation when he got the call. "To me it was an honour in itself, just to be asked."

Heward made the team, the only non-NHL roster player to make it, playing every game on his way to the gold medal. Not bad for a guy who had trouble finding a regular spot in the NHL only a couple of seasons earlier.

He would also be on Team Canada in 2004 for its gold medal in Prague, although he played less that year. "The second one was a little different. I didn't get to play every game," he said.

Heward's ice time diminished with the arrival of Scott Niedermayer. "It's not all that shameful losing your spot to a guy like that," he said. At something like the World Championships, players do what they must to help the team. "There are so many different roles guys have to accept. We were playing for our country, and no if, ands or buts, you do what you have to [do] to win...I loved every minute of it."

That's not surprising for a player who has seen the lows of the game against which to measure a high such as a gold medal. "Hockey is a game that can turn you upside down, and then right you the next minute," he said, "It's like being on a rough sea. You just want to keep it on an even keel the best you can."

Heward said the World Championships were the high, and brought into focus an injury when he was only 21 that had doctors saying he'd never play hockey again. "I remember sitting in the hospital going through rehab wondering if I'd ever skate again, and wondering what I was going to do if I never played again."

But Heward persevered, returned to hockey, and years later all the sweat and effort paid off with the gold medals. "There's going to be a wall in my basement just devoted to Team Canada. We get to keep our jerseys, and there's the medals."

And if he ever gets the call again, Heward will be quick to add to his memorabilia collection. "I'd pay them to play. There are just so many things that go through your mind. It's a great experience."

The World Championships, though, were a long way from how Heward started his career back home in Saskatchewan. Heward was another of those players who progressed through the Regina system to play not only his minor hockey in his hometown, but junior as well, although he almost had to travel north to Prince Albert for that. "I was initially listed by the Prince Albert Raiders," he said, adding that was an important step for him as a young player. "When I was first listed by a WHL team, that's when I started to think I might be good enough to play major junior."

Heward admitted he had been a local WHL fan though. "The Pats had always been my favourite team, but when you get listed you end up with another favourite team pretty quickly."

Heward said at one time he had sort of wished he had to move away to play junior just for the experience, but time has changed that view. "Looking back I'm so happy having played my whole time in my hometown. Being a 16-year-old kid and having to move away from home is not an experience you want to wish on a lot of people. It's tough."

That being said, Heward's years as a Pat were not that successful team-wise. "We were not probably the best team around," he admitted with a laugh. "We had some decent years. We ended up getting to the second round of the playoffs once.

"My four years there we went through a lot of players. We just never found the right chemistry."

As a Pat, Heward at least found some chemistry in his first season lining up with Frank Kovacs and Mike Sillinger as the "Pup line," three 16-year-olds, all from Regina.

If Heward's time as a Pat was a bit rocky, he was still viewed well by the pros, going 16th overall in the 1989 draft to the Pittsburgh Penguins. As a first-round selection, one might have expected smooth sailing ahead for the talented forward, but that wasn't to be. The Penguins had different ideas of where Heward would fit into their program. After his draft year, they moved Heward to defence and the transition was a tough one. "It was really tough on me. I had just been drafted as a right winger, but the Penguins and Pats thought I would be more useful to the team, and maybe to the Pittsburgh Penguin organization by making the move."

In Junior Heward said he made the transition work. "I got by in Junior on instinct and what I had seen other guys do, and my ability to skate." That wasn't going to be enough as he turned pro, spending his first season with the Muskegon Lumberjacks. "When I first turned pro it [the move to defence] made things a lot more difficult than I wanted it to be. It made it a lot more difficult starting my pro career."

The things Heward had done as a Pat to compensate for his move to the blueline were suddenly no longer enough to get by. "At that level it's a lot more of a talent game, where you have to read situations and react to them. I was still used to scoring at all costs."

Heward said the scoring motivation had to be put on the backburner as he learned a different role on the fly. It was a transition that has him proudly calling himself a journeyman player as he looks back on his career.

At the same time it was a career Heward admits almost ended prematurely. Things were not progressing in the minors as he had envisioned they would, and a career away from the ice started to look good to him. Then fate played a card. "The thing that happened to me was the NHL lock-out," he said.

With no NHL to play, Heward came into contact with Tom Rennie with the Canadian National Team program.

"In a matter of three days I was signed and part of the program, and that saved my career," said Heward. "I was a career minor league player at that point."

Heward admitted he struggled to adapt to a new role amid the pressures of professional hockey, where one needs near nightly success to please the coaches and scouts within an organization.

The National Team program took a decidedly different approach. The program was designed to let players grow into their roles. "They [the National Team] only scheduled a little over 50 games. We were a touring team, and spent a good part of the year just practicing," said Heward. "We were watching videos and learning the technical side of things. I had no choice but to get better." It was a system that Heward said nurtured a player's development. "Your confidence level and your skill level just increase 100-fold.

"I didn't have to worry about GMs and scouts evaluating every night...And you were playing as hard as you could for your country."

Heward said the program was geared toward a goal down the road, so the team might lose 7-2 on a given night, and the coaches would still be pleased if they saw players getting better in certain aspects of their game, because that would help achieve the long range goals of the program.

The experience sharpened his skills to the point that when the NHL lock-out ended, the Toronto Maple Leafs came calling, and he was able to live the dream of many from the Canadian Prairies. "I played in the old Maple Leaf Gardens, which I had grown up dreaming about," he said. It and the Montreal Forum were long the Meccas of kids playing street hockey.

It might have been hockey at Maple Leaf Gardens, but it wasn't the success many expected of the Leafs of that era—1995–1997. "We had a lot of good players," said Heward. "We had good nights, and we had bad nights, but something just wasn't right."

Even with the likes of Mats Sundin, Doug Gilmour and Saskatchewan alumni Wendel Clark and Garth Butcher, the Leafs just couldn't jell to make a run at the Stanley Cup, although at the time Heward was just happy to have finally arrived in "The Show." "Your first year in the NHL, you're just like a kid," he said.

What would lie ahead for Heward professionally was a career that saw him well-travelled. There were stints in expansion cities such as Nashville and Columbus, plus a stop with the New York Islanders. In each city he was a player often shuffled between the big club and its top minor league affiliate.

Along the way Heward made use of his time in the minors, being named the Best Defenceman with the Philadelphia

Phantoms in 1997–98, and also winning the Calder Cup in 1998, which opened the door to Nashville. "It was the first championship I'd ever won," he said, looking at that as the silver lining of not playing in the NHL that year.

Looking back, Heward thought at times he was on the verge of a more-extended visit to the NHL, in going to the expansion Predators, for example. "I thought I was going to get an opportunity to play more," he said, but his time in a Predator uniform was only 63 games for the 1998–99 season.

Heward said the expansion team was better than anyone expected. "The first year we won more games than we won my first year in Toronto," he said. "We surprised a lot of teams."

It was a case of several guys whom other teams had given up on, leaving them unprotected in the expansion draft and coming together to show they still had something left. "We worked hard and ended up winning games," said Heward. "It was a great experience. Nashville was a really nice place to play. Hockey was new, but they were excited about it," he said. "... There was no expectations, no pressure on us."

It was also interesting to find that as players they were celebrities to many Nashville performers. Heward was of course familiar with the likes of Vince Gill and Martina McBride. "They'd come down to the dressing rooms and want our autograph. That was a pretty good feeling."

It was a similar feeling in Columbus when Heward joined the expansion Blue Jackets in 2000. "There were no expectations or pressure there either," said Heward. Again the team exceeded most people's dreams, setting a new record for points by an expansion team set by Philadelphia in 1967–68. For Heward, the season was also special because it reunited him with old junior buddy Mike Sillinger. "It was the first time in my NHL career I got to play with him, and he's one of my best friends," he said.

But after the 2002 season ended in Columbus, Heward decided it was time to change gears in his career. While he said he could have tried to hook up with yet another NHL team or take a minor deal to play his way back to the big league, "I just wasn't interested in doing that again." Instead, Heward packed his bags and headed to Europe to start a new career in the game.

Heward said there are no regrets about his NHL experience. "I had a good career in the NHL. I had done a lot more than I thought I would." That being said, the move to Europe was most likely the best thing he did, as his World Championships attest. He also likes the environment in which his hockey is played.

"[Switzerland], it's good. I wouldn't say it's great hockey. The Swiss aren't quite as into the game as Canadians or some other European countries, but the quality of life is good here…The hockey over here is better than the American Hockey League. It may not be as tough, but there are better players."

"I want to play over here as long as I can, maybe another three or four years," he said in early 2005.

A Proud Hockey Journey

For Bill Hicke hockey became something of a circular path. A native of Regina, Hicke played through the minor hockey system, proudly wearing the Regina Pats jersey through to junior. Then, following a professional career which would encompass 15 years, Hicke would return to the Queen City and become part owner of the Pats of the Western Hockey League.

It's not too surprising Hicke's hockey path went as it did, since the game and the city were so intertwined for him as a youth. "We used to live in the north end of Regina, and my older brother [John] was a pretty good hockey player, and I used to follow him around," he said. "We used to go all the way down to Exhibition Stadium to play."

At a young age, Hicke said he wanted to be like his older brother, but at times came up short. "Both of us tried out for the Bantam team. He made it, and I didn't," he said. He was two years younger. The next year, however, Hicke made the team, and never looked back. "I went on from there to play 11 years with the Regina Pats."

As a Pat, Hicke recalled winning championships from Bantam through Juvenile. "I was fortunate enough to play on teams that were really good," he said.

Eventually Hicke's own talents would take him to the Junior Pats, then playing in the Saskatchewan Junior Hockey League, where in 1957–58 he recorded 58 goals and 97 points, under Pat coach Murray Armstrong.

At the time the Montreal Canadiens of the NHL provided "about 100 per cent of the sponsorship," for the Pats and that meant players on the team belonged to the big club. "You never had a chance. If you were good enough to play pro, you were invited to the Montreal camp."

For Hicke, the invitation came down from Conn Smythe, and he headed east to training camp at an age most players are still playing minor. "I went to camp when I was 15. Murray Balfour and I took the train. It took us three-and-a-half days to get there. The train stopped everywhere, six or seven hours in Moosomin alone." The trip was fun, but he would come back alone, as Montreal kept Balfour, assigning him to the Ottawa-Hull Junior team.

Hicke and Balfour would reunite as the two became teammates in Rochester in Hicke's rookie season in the American Hockey League. "He [Balfour] was my roommate," he said. Balfour was a tough, rugged player in his day, who died at the young age of 49. "What a terrible tragedy."

For Hicke, his first season in the AHL, 1958–59, was memorable, as he scored 97 points to lead the league, while earning the Les Cunningham Award as league Most Valuable Player, the Dudley (Red) Garrett Memorial Award as Rookie of the Year and the John B. Sollenberger Trophy as top regular season scorer.

"I had a helluva year, but I had lots of help, which you've got to have," said Hicke.

It was the kind of year that gets you noticed by the big club in the NHL, and when Rochester fell from the playoff picture, Hicke was called up for the playoffs with the Canadiens, going all the way to a Stanley Cup championship. "That was something you wouldn't expect," he said of the quick championship. It was his first sweet taste in the NHL, and started a stint which saw him play over six seasons with the Habs, including capturing a second Cup in 1960.

It wasn't exactly the best situation for the young Hicke to skate into. His arrival in Montreal ran parallel to the retirement in 1960 of Maurice "Rocket" Richard, an icon of the game in Montreal for years. The Rocket's leaving left a large hole on the club's roster, and in the hearts of fans who sought a replacement. Coming off the rookie year Hicke had in the AHL, he received billing as the heir to the "Rocket."

There was little Hicke could do to fill such historic skates. In his first season, covering 43 games, he scored only three goals, growing that to 18 and 20 the next two years. Modest numbers when compared to the great Richard.

While his career in Montreal got off to a slower start than he may have wished for, Hicke said he just appreciated being in the NHL. "I think when you are the age I was, the most amazing thing was how good all the players were," he said.

One player who stood out was Jean Beliveau, and not only for the way he played. "I sat beside Beliveau and he was just a complete gentleman."

While Hicke said he appreciated the talent level, fitting in was not easy. "They had one helluva team," he said, adding language was the barrier. "People don't talk about it much, but there were only three or four guys that could speak English on the team."

Regardless of the language of players, Hicke said Montreal was the cream of the NHL at the time, being in the midst of five straight Stanley Cup wins. "You look at the nine best players in the league, we had seven of them," he said, pointing to the likes of Bernie "Boom-Boom" Geoffrion, Henri Richard and Dick Moore. "I'd say we had five guys better than any other team except maybe Detroit who had Gordie Howe and Ted Lindsay."

Hicke said Montreal was so offensively talented at the time, they forced a fundamental change in the game. Teams had stayed a man short for a full two minutes when someone took a minor penalty, but when Montreal often scored two, and even three goals in such situations, the league made it so the penalized player returned to the ice after a goal was scored.

By 1964 though, Hicke could see he no longer fit into the Canadiens' formula, as his bench time grew. He requested a trade and was soon on his way to the New York Rangers. After a stint in New York, Hicke was on the move again, joining the Oakland Golden Seals when the league expanded from six to 12 teams for the 1967–68 season. The California experience was an interesting one, he said. "It was different. The first night we played there, the game was almost canceled because two-thirds of the guys had sunburn. They fell asleep at the pool."

The expansion Seals actually had a decent club in their first season. "We just didn't play as good as we should have," said Hicke, pointing out the team had the likes of veterans Billy Harris, Bobby Baun and Bert Marshall. Even with players with such experience, the Seals won only 15 games and finished last in the six-team expansion division. For his part, Hicke finished third in team scoring, with 44 points.

While Hicke had followed in his older brother John's footsteps as a youngster, John never did play pro hockey, which surprised Bill, considering his brother was six feet tall, and he was only five-foot-eight. Looking back, Bill said it was the reality of life that got in John's way. "In those days we never had very much money," said Bill, a situation that forced John into the workforce at 16.

At the same time though, Bill's younger brother Ernie would follow him to the NHL, playing in 502 regular season games. Ernie would actually join Bill in Oakland for the 1970–71 season, although the brothers rarely played on a line together. In both 1968 and 1969, Hicke made the NHL All Star game representing the Seals.

Hicke stayed in Oakland until 1971, had a cup of coffee in Pittsburgh and then was back in the minors until he gave the pros one more shot with the Alberta Oilers of the World Hockey Association. After a single WHA season, asthma finally caught up with Hicke and he retired. "I had a bad case of asthma and just couldn't play anymore."

In retirement Hicke returned to Regina, started a business, and was soon once again a Regina Pat, this time as part-owner. He and partners Morley Gusway and Ted Knight purchased the Pats in 1986, owning the WHL franchise for 11 seasons before selling it to Russ and Diane Parker.

Hicke served as the Pats Governor from '86 through '88, then took over as team general manager from 1989 to 1996, also coaching in 1993–94. "I had to make a change, and as it happened I took them to the finals," he said of the coaching stint.

For Hicke, team ownership was a definite thrill, but not one that came close to playing the game. "Playing in the NHL is a dream every kid who laces up his skates dreams about, and it just doesn't happen that often," he said. "... With junior hockey it's just different. It's a lot of fun, but it's not playing."

Still it was his ownership of the Pats that earned him one of the biggest honours from hockey. In 2004, he was named as one of four recipients of a WHL Governors Award. The award recognizes outstanding achievements in the game, service to the league, and contributions to the overall growth and development of the WHL. In the case of the WHL award, it was special as it was presented at centre ice at a Pats game. "I was nervous. It was the largest crowd they had this year. My family was there. It was pretty emotional."

The award came after another honour Hicke is proud of, induction into the Saskatchewan Sports Hall of Fame.

For a kid from Regina, it has been a hockey journey of many highs, starting and ending as a Pat. "I consider myself very, very lucky. It's been fun, and I'm proud of it, and ending up back in Regina where my family is."

A Man Who Spoke His Mind

Grit and perseverance might best describe the way Bobby Schmautz approached the game of hockey. Schmautz grew up learning the game from his father Pete and brothers Cliff, Arnie and Kenny. "I started back in Saskatoon. My dad used to build us a rink in the back." Even his sisters got into the skating sports, with Jeannette teaching figure skating in Saskatoon as an adult, and his late sister Eunice being a speed skater in her day.

The basic skills developed on the backyard rink, and Schmautz moved into organized hockey, moving up through the minor system in the bridge city, until his junior days with the Saskatoon Blades of the Saskatchewan Junior Hockey League. He earned Rookie of the Year honours his first season.

In his final season, 1963–64, Schmautz scored 55 goals and 98 points, good enough to get him a tryout with the Los Angeles Blades of the old Western Hockey League. He would join brothers Cliff and Arnie in the WHL, actually facing off against them when they played for Portland and he was in LA. Cliff would also see NHL time in Philly.

At the time Schmautz said the WHL was a league close to the National Hockey League in its level of play. "The WHL was an awful good hockey league," he said, "When the NHL expanded, teams like Vancouver and Portland could have moved over and been competitive."

Schmautz would wear the Blades uniform until the team folded from the league, and he found his rights were suddenly the property of the NHL's Chicago Blackhawks. "Chicago had first rights on anybody who played on the Blades in Saskatoon," he said.

The Hawks would assign Schmautz to Dallas of the old Central Hockey League, and after a season-and-a-half, he would finally break into the NHL. "Now that was a dream come true," he said.

At the time the Hawks were deep in talent, with the likes of Bobby Hull and Stan Mikita, and ice time for a rookie was at a premium. Guys like Mikita and Ken Wharram "took us rookies under their wings and treated us very well," but Schmautz was unhappy with his playing time. It didn't help that things were never smooth with Chicago coach Billy Reay. "Young guys didn't get along well with Reay," he said.

Schmautz recalled one night when he was lined up with Bobby Hull and scored twice while adding an assist. "The next night I didn't even dress," he said.

Never one to remain quiet in the face of perceived trouble, Schmautz voiced his displeasure. "I was very happy to get back to the minors again where I could play."

The trip back to the minors settled Schmautz back in the WHL, this time with the Seattle Totems. It would be two more seasons before the rugged forward finally broke in to stay in the NHL with the Vancouver Canucks.

Schmautz admits it was a long haul to the NHL, but extended minor league time was not unusual in those days. "Everybody today figures they can play, and so do the scouts. It was completely different then," he said. "... The problem was getting ice time in the old days. Teams all had their veterans and they went with the old guys no matter what."

The Canucks would keep Schmautz through parts of four seasons, watching him blossom as a player. In 1972–73, he scored 38 goals and 71 points, while racking up 137 penalty minutes, leading the team in all three categories. He was on a line with Andre Boudrias, who finished with 70 points, and Don Tannahill, who had 43.

In some respects Schmautz was most proud of his tenacious nature, which racked up the penalty minutes. "In those days if you had more than 100 minutes in penalties you were a player because you had to play to get them. They were honest penalties that happened during the game. For me that says something."

While such numbers might have been the start of a long career on Canada's West Coast, a trade was instead in the offing, and Schmautz said it was the biggest break of his career. "Going from Vancouver to Boston was probably the best point in my career," he said. "The first year in Boston we lost out in the finals 1–0 to Philadelphia. The next six years we'd lose out again to Chicago then Montreal and Montreal."

It was great success, as along the way Schmautz rolled through seven consecutive 20-plus goal seasons. He would have traded a season or two of the goals to have bagged one Stanley Cup. "I would have loved to have had a Stanley Cup. Afterwards I used to tell Henri Richard [who had multiple Cup wins in Montreal] he could have let us have at least one."

In 1977, Schmautz had a notable playoff run on a personal level, scoring 11 goals in only 14 games. Looking back he said not a lot of players hit that figure, even today. "And I played on the power play when Bobby Orr was still playing, so I must have been pretty good."

Playing in Boston also put Schmautz on the team with the best player he ever played with. "Bobby Orr was still there," he said. The Bruins were deep in players destined for the Hall of Fame, including Phil Esposito, Gerry Cheevers, John Bucyk, and they traded to bring in Brad Park and Jean Ratelle. Bucyk became Schmautz's linemate and lifelong friend, completing a trio which included fellow Saskatchewanite Gregg Sheppard. "Chief [Bucyk] was such a great guy. He pretty well held the team together off the ice. He definitely took care of the young guys…I still talk to Chief quite often."

The time in Boston also brought into being a lasting friendship with one of hockey's most colourful characters, Don Cherry. "I became real good friends with Grapes," he said. The two had actually met in the minors when Schmautz played seven games with the Rochester Americans.

Schmautz said he appreciated Cherry as a coach, but it was that support of his coach that pushed him out of Boston when Cherry and Bruins General Manager Harry Sinden were at loggerheads. "They were struggling over whose team it was. On some points Cherry was right, and on some points he was wrong," said Schmautz. "But Cherry backed his players and we backed him."

As veteran players looked to Schmautz for comment, he made his opinion known. "I made some statements. I was traded.

"I probably should have kept my mouth shut and played my last two or three years in Boston. That might have been the right thing for me, and my career."

That is in retrospect. At the time Schmautz was off to Edmonton. It was only for 29 games, but it was an opportunity to rub shoulder pads with two more stars of the game, Wayne Gretzky and Mark Messier. "They were just starting out," he said.

The stay with the Oilers was short, as Schmautz sought a trade to the Colorado Rockies, where Cherry was on the bench. "They traded me to Colorado. It could have been because I went to practice [in Edmonton] one day wearing a Colorado jersey," he said with a laugh.

After only 20 games with the Rockies, he was released, and it looked as though his career was over. He had a tryout with Boston on coach Gerry Cheevers, but he knew that was going nowhere in spite of leading camp in goals. "[Harry] Sinden wasn't going to sign me, but we gave it a try," he said.

Retirement loomed until Jake Milford of the Canucks called. Schmautz was about to return to the B.C. city where he owned a home, so he signed on to once again play with the Canucks. It looked like he was set for a good run in Vancouver for a second time. "I was always taught it was important to win, and we were winning. I was on a 30-goal pace, and then I was told I couldn't play the game anymore.

"I just said that's enough. I'm fed up. I'm fed up with the game I gave a lot to... There didn't seem to be any honour by the teams that you did something for."

In 1981, Schmautz moved away from hockey completely, joining his brother in business in Portland.

Looking back, Schmautz knows he was often outspoken, and that was the case with Canucks coach Harry Neale in his final season. It was a case of commenting on things to do with the team that Neale didn't like listening to. Although he spoke out, it was with the right intentions. "When I had something to say it was for the betterment of the team, not the betterment of Bobby Schmautz."

Looking back on a career that spanned more than 800 regular and playoff games in the NHL, Schmautz said ultimately he leaves comparisons to those he played with and against. "It's the respect you get from your peers, the guys you played against and with which sums up the significance of your career," he said, noting he had longevity. "It wasn't just a cup of coffee. There was a time it looked like it might just be a cup of coffee, but I ended up playing a lot of years."

It's About Hard Work

Playing more than 1,000 games in the National Hockey League was never really on the mind of Jim Neilson when he was young, but that's exactly where hockey would take him.

As a youngster Neilson felt he was a good player, but never really looked to the pros. "When I was playing Pee Wee hockey I thought I was pretty good. We had one of the better teams in the school league, but I wasn't thinking of the NHL." Those thoughts would emerge later, after a less than typical youth for Neilson, who is of First Nations descent. He was born in Big River, but left that Saskatchewan community at a young age, growing up in Prince Albert. It was not a youth Neilson might have picked though, spending his formative years at St. Patrick's Orphanage— a basically white orphanage—along with his two younger sisters.

"I got my Grades 1 to 8 at the orphanage," he said. From there he attended St. Mary's School to complete Grades 9 to 12. "You had to be a good student. There weren't too many distractions around," he said. In addition to school classes, Neilson learned something else that turned out equally important to the youngster. "That's where I learned to skate, at the orphanage," he said.

In the earliest days, Neilson's hockey was focused on the school league, but he would soon progress to one of the best-known hockey programs in Saskatchewan at the time, that of the Prince Albert Mintos. His time with the Junior Mintos was where he first realized he might take hockey further than local play. The New York Rangers at the time sponsored the Mintos and that made all the players Ranger property. They signed Neilson to a contract. "Then I had an idea I could keep going," he said. "I had an idea I could step up to another league."

Along the way Neilson made a positional change too. "I had been playing forward most of my life through school," he said. He was eventually put back on the blueline. He said the move proved a good one, and he settled in because he could skate backwards pretty well. "That stuff was just what you did when they told you to do it."

Neilson credits playing as a kid with the ability to adapt so easily. In the orphanage, after breakfast, at noon and after school, he played hockey. "I got oodles of ice time," and that is where his skills sharpened. He would have 25 minutes and the goal was to keep the puck away from other kids, "so you were skating, and turning left, and turning right. You were learning to play the game."

Neilson's first professional stop was in the Eastern Professional Hockey League with the Kitchener-Waterloo Beavers in 1961–62. It was a stop with a team filled with faces which would become familiar to Neilson in the ensuing years, as well as to fans of the NHL. Teammates included the likes of Jean Ratelle, Rod Gilbert and fellow Saskatchewanite Dave Balon of Wakaw.

Neilson fit right in, earning Rookie of the Year honours in

his first EPHL season, although again he never thought too much about things. "I just never even really thought about it, I just knew I'd come up the ladder," he said. When you win a Rookie of the Year award, though, that tends to draw attention from higher up in the organization, and for Neilson that meant attending training camp with the big club in New York.

New York was a bit different from Prince Albert in the early 1960s, but Neilson said he took the culture shock pretty much in stride. "I had been to the Ranger camp the previous fall. The next year I made the jump to the NHL," he said.

Amid the tall buildings and aura of Madison Square Garden, he drew on his youth experiences to keep him centered. "I grew up in an orphanage," he reminded. That toughened him in some ways. "So I never got too overwhelmed by it [New York]."

Neilson said he also focused on learning from those around him with the Rangers, in particular veteran rearguard Harry Howell. "I kept an eye on solid guys like that who had been there," he said. "I kind of learned by watching them. "I didn't want to just sit there and gawk at the big buildings."

Like playing at the orphanage, where he learned by doing, Neilson tried to keep the mind set as a pro too. "You try to improve every little skill as you go," he said. "There's a heckuva a lot of reward in just hard work."

In Neilson's first National Hockey League season he'd dress for 69 games, although in the first half the season his ice time was pretty limited. As the season progressed, though, he settled into a more regular shift with the Rangers. He said it helped that expectations for him were not too high. "There weren't a lot of press clippings in front of me to live up to," he said.

Neilson's career was given an early push when he was teamed with Howell as a defensive pairing, although he would spend much of his Ranger career lined up with Rod Seiling.

The pairing, which lasted for some nine seasons, was somewhat unusual, admitted Neilson, since both looked after their own end first. "We were both kind of the same type. We'd get the puck and pass it out," he said. "We were stay-at-home type defenceman. Our job was to protect the goalie. It was our job to get the puck and get it going back the other way in a hurry."

While Neilson played against greats such as Gordie Howe, he wasn't the hardest to defend against on the ice. That honour, in Neilson's mind fell to players such as Dave Keon and Stan Mikita. "They could turn on a dime. They were just like a bug on water. They were hard to contain."

For the next dozen years, and more than 800 games, he would patrol the New York blueline. "We still had a pretty good team, a lot of good talent," he said, pointing to a list of Ranger teammates that included Ratelle, Gilbert, Vic Hadfield, Keith Tkachuk, goaltender Ed Giacomin and fellow defenceman Brad Park.

As good as the Rangers were, a Stanley Cup eluded Neilson, who made the finals only once. "It's a tough grind just to make the Stanley Cup," he said. The year he made it they faced the Boston Bruins with Bobby Orr and goaltender "Gerry Cheevers at his best."

The string of seasons was impressive, although it was not something Neilson dwelled on, accepting late career moves that saw him spend two seasons as a California Seal, two as a Cleveland Baron, and winding up in Edmonton, then of the World Hockey Association, for his final year.

"I enjoyed my years in Oakland very much," he said. He didn't find the move after all his years in New York that difficult. "You got out to golf a lot. It wasn't as intense as New York," he said with a laugh. With the Rangers there was always scrutiny but with the long-defunct Seals, hockey "was the third page of sports, so it was buried."

When California became Cleveland, the situation became harder as a player. "It was a tough two years there," he said, noting they often played games in front of only 4,000 fans. "People never took to us, but we never had a very good team either."

For his last move to Edmonton, Neilson was lured by former Ranger teammate Glen Sather, by then in management with the Oilers.

Neilson remembered "Slats" the player for his grit. "He was one of the guys who would jump off the bench and stir things up," he said.

Neilson's season would be limited to only 35 games as injuries caught up with the 17-year veteran. "It was part of the hockey journey," he said of the jump to the WHA. He did get a chance to play closer to Prince Albert, and to play with Wayne Gretzky with the move.

It wasn't until after his NHL career that Neilson came to realize he had become something of a role model for First Nations players. In his younger years his background was not really understood, growing up in the predominantly white orphanage. As he aged he started to learn about his heritage, but in school even family connections were minimal. "I had my two sisters but I really only saw them passing in the halls."

Today Neilson talks to Aboriginal community groups, but added there are "a lot of younger players kids relate to now." At the same time many older fans still remember his career, which wrapped up in 1979. The message is simple when he speaks. "For the hockey part, and anything in life in general, it's about hard work...It's about feeling good about yourself."

Gals Find Success Within Hounds Tradition

Notre Dame College at Wilcox is arguably the best-known hockey factory in Saskatchewan, and perhaps Canada. That being the case it should come as little surprise that the Hounds of Notre Dame were quick to add women's hockey to their roster of school teams. "We would have had a full time (girls) hockey team by 1990-'91," said Eric Lockwood, who coached the Midget girls team from 1993 through to 2005.

His final year proved a special one, as the team won the inaugural Mac's Tournament for Midget girls' hockey. Long recognized as a premier Midget tournament attracting teams from across Canada and abroad, it was the first time a girl's division was part of the mix in Calgary.

"The Mac's has a great reputation as a tournament," said Lockwood. "It's a great high profile event girls can now go to to get experience."

The first girls' event saw 12 teams involved from Western Canada, including three clubs from Saskatchewan. Lockwood said he expects you'll see teams drawn from further afield in the near future. "I expect a lot more of a mix as they move forward," he said, noting eight teams were drawn from Alberta in the first year.

For a first-year event, Lockwood said the tournament was a good calibre. "It was pretty exciting. Our round robin games were pretty darned good."

The Hounds played three games in the round robin, and their coach said the Hounds "got a bit better as we went on." The improvement was a good thing because it helped ready Notre Dame to face Bowness, a team from Alberta. "It was maybe the best game I ever coached in as a girls coach," said Lockwood. "We were down 2–0 going into the third period."

In the third the Hounds clawed back into it, then gave up a short-handed goal to still trail by one late in the frame. "We pulled the goaltender and got a goal with 30 seconds left," said Lockwood. That sent the game to overtime, and it wasn't until the second extra frame that the Hounds found the winner.

"It was a great game, just back and forth," said Lockwood.

Tegan Schroeder was on defence on the winning Hounds, and she too felt the game was the high point of her hockey, even without receiving a trophy or medal at its conclusion.

"It was really exciting," said the-then Grade 11 student. "Our team had just come off our Christmas break. We hadn't practiced or anything in a long time. After the break we just all sort of met up in Calgary, and we played really well."

In the case of the Bowness game, Schroeder said the two teams had something of a rivalry going over the course of the season. As the game moved into the third, with the Hounds trailing, and then into sudden death overtime, Schroeder said the team just tried to stay focused on executing on the ice. "We told ourselves we can't just say we're going out there and doing it. You have to go out and actually do it," she said. "You can't just talk the talk, you have to walk the walk."

As the game wore on, Schroeder said it became a major goal just to keep skating, as fatigue set in. "It was tough. Some players got double-shifts, but you just had to keep going and going."

When the red light for the Hounds goal went on, "it was crazy," said Schroeder. "We were more excited than when we won the final."

Hayley Klassen assisted on the tying goal as the seconds ticked down in the third period, then netted the winner in the second overtime. "As soon as I scored it I was leaning against the boards and everybody was jumping around me," she said. She was almost too tired to cheer. "But, the feeling inside was that we'd accomplished something great."

Klassen said the Hounds had sort of an ace-in-the-hole as overtime loomed. Most of the girls had family in the stands and as they hit the ice for every period, their fans cheering in a rink so far from home helped keep them going.

The fact the Hounds had fought back from 2–0, and then overcome the late Bowness short-handed goal, also fired Klassen, who remembered telling the others in the dressing room, "we have worked so hard, we can't lose in overtime now."

In Klassen's mind the game was the highlight, not only of the Mac's Tournament, but of the entire Notre Dame season. "It was probably the best game of our season. When you win in double overtime, not a lot can beat that."

Of course from Klassen's perspective the entire tournament was a great experience, and a step for female hockey. "It was exciting. It was a really good tournament. There was a lot of publicity for the girls, not just about the guys."

That set up the Hounds in the Mac's final, a game they won 4–2 over the Calgary NEAA (North East Athletic Association)

Flyers. "It was a little bit anticlimactic, not to take anything away from the team we played, but coming off that overtime game," said Lockwood.

It was also a game of perseverance for the Hounds, who stepped on the finals' ice less than 24 hours after the Bowness game. "We got up early and sort of hung on in the third period," said Lockwood. "It wasn't pretty, that's for sure."

Schroeder said the win was in part overshadowed by sheer tiredness. "We'd put everything into that overtime game," she said. "Fatigue really hurt us [in the final]. We were so tired, but we didn't let up too much."

That was certainly the case for Schroeder personally, as she was named Most Valuable Player in the final game. She was modest about the award, suggesting when someone got into trouble, someone else was always there to help them out, and she simply was the one who got the nod for the MVP.

While the female Hounds are now enjoying success in hockey, Lockwood said there is a long history of ice sports for girls at the school. Prior to girl's hockey at Notre Dame, the school iced ringette teams, but over time the switch was made to hockey. He said the move simply followed a rather general trend in girls' sports.

"I just think it was viewed as hockey was the coming thing," he said. In his opinion hockey has proven the right choice. "I am not one to make up a different game just for girls. If you want to play hockey—play hockey."

Certainly the game of hockey has grown quickly as a women's sport, powered by the ingrained love of the game all Canadians seem to share. Still, how the game has developed has been surprising in Lockwood's mind. "I'm a little surprised in that it's happened pretty quickly," he said. "The ability of players has improved pretty quickly, especially in the last five years."

Asked if he had an idea why the game has caught on so well with women, Lockwood went to some of the basics of hockey. "It's just a fun game to play," he said. Like men, women like the physical nature of the game and the energy of it. Of course the game has been spurred on by events such as Team Canada winning gold in women's hockey at the 2002 Olympic Games in Salt Lake City. "I think that was huge," said Lockwood. "It really put the women's game kind of on a parallel with the men."

Lockwood said the Canadian team faced a lot of adversity leading up to, and through the Olympics, "and they didn't collapse. They struggled through it, and won it." Such effort endeared the team to young girl hockey players, and the rest of Canada.

It didn't hurt the aura of the women's game to see the obvious support of the men's team, loaded with the biggest names in the game, at the gold medal game cheering on the women, said Lockwood. When someone like Mario Lemieux speaks highly of the game, people listen. "It put the women's game on a bit of a pedestal, higher than it had been before," said Lockwood. "Young girls saw that all happening, and said they wanted to be part of it."

Schroeder was one of many who look to Team Canada star Hayley Wickenheiser, also from Saskatchewan, as a role model "She's the one. She has family in my town, her grandpa, and he talks to me," she said.

As Team Canada was going for gold in Salt Lake City Schroeder was on the ice in Humboldt playing on the Zone 5 team going for the bronze medal in the Saskatchewan Winter Games. "We were kind of doing the same thing at the same time, just a few levels lower for me," said Schroeder, who won the bronze and got back to her room just in time to see the end of the Team Canada victory.

Lockwood has seen the game's growth standing behind the bench at Notre Dame for a dozen years.

"My first team, I basically had three top quality hockey players," he said. That included Delaney Collins, who was the last cut for Salt Lake City, and Carol Scheibel, again a late cut of Team Canada for the Olympics in Nagano, and goaltender Tamara Andre. While the three stand-outs anchored the team, the rest of Lockwood's first team were not nearly as hockey-oriented. "It was a good complimentary cast, but some had never played before, and some has just moved over from ringette."

Jump ahead to 2005, and the depth of talent is far deeper on the women's side. "Now every one of the girls started playing at a young age," said Lockwood. Most also have aspirations of taking their hockey farther. In 2005, Lockwood's Midget team would graduate nine girls, and he said at least seven were likely to play college hockey. With the growth of women's hockey at the college level in both Canada, and the United States, young players have "lots of opportunity" to turn their ice skills into further education.

Klassen was in Grade 12 as the Hounds won the inaugural Mac's Tournament, and was headed to Ohio State University to play college hockey after graduation. She said it has always been her goal to play college hockey. "It should be a good experience for me. They have a really good hockey program."

In many ways Klassen's hockey path follows the well-worn pattern male players have used for years. She began playing the game in her hometown of Warman when she was four. "I think just because my brother played." However the game soon held her interest on its own. "It's intense. It's always changing on the ice. It's exciting," she offered.

While most girls now have female role models to fashion their careers in the game around, Klassen still points to the brother she followed into the game. She said she's always watching game films of Chad, who played in the Western Hockey League with the Spokane Chiefs. "I'm always trying to get a little more like him."

Schroeder is somewhat typical of the current Hounds too as a hockey player. "I started skating when I was three and playing hockey when I was five or six. I started playing with the boys. I played nine years with them," she said.

When she started in the game in her hometown of Lumsden, it was play with the guys or not at all, since there were no girls' teams, although that has changed too, she said.

For Schroeder, becoming a hockey player was simply natural. "There's so many great opportunities. It helps you grow as a person. You meet so many great people," she said. Down the road, Schroeder wants that college opportunity. "I've had a few colleges talk to me," she said.

The new depth of talent and greater dedication to the game from a young age opens doors for Lockwood as a coach. "You can do so much more with them. I really don't coach these girls any different than I would a guy's team."

With the growth of women's hockey, Lockwood sees more doors, like the establishment of a women's division at the Mac's Tournament, opening. As it stands, the Western Canadian Shield is the highest goal for a Midget club team, but he said in his mind a national championship "much like the Telus Cup for guys" is likely within five years.

"Wait Till They Drop the Puck"

Bo Jackson and Deion Sanders have become household names in the sporting world because of their prowess in two sports.

Before either was born, Canada had its own two-sport star—Gerry James. James, a Hall of Famer for his gridiron talents in the Canadian Football league, also suited up for five seasons with the Toronto Maple Leafs of the National Hockey League. Playing for the Winnipeg Blue Bombers from 1953 to 1960, James won the first ever Schenley Award as the league's most outstanding Canadian in 1954, and again in 1957. He was also nominated in 1955 and 1960. James was on the Blue Bomber Grey Cup-winning team in 1959 and 1960.

His hockey career was less impressive, amassing only 149 games, 14 goals, 40 points and 257 penalty minutes while a Leaf. Had he been a better hockey player, maybe he would have been recognized for his two-sport career, said James while signing autographs at a card show in Yorkton, Saskatchewan, a few years ago.

"Let's face facts, I wasn't a great hockey player. I didn't have great talent. I was there to enforce other people's right," said James—a clear reference to his time spent in the sin bin.

"It wasn't as if I was a 30- or 40-goal scorer, like these guys who are good baseball players and good football players. I didn't have the same impact. I was the 18th guy on a 17 player roster, just sort of hanging on by my fingernails," he said, gripping the edge of the table.

James may have only hung on by his fingernails, but he knew from a young age playing for the Leafs was his dream. Born in Regina, James actually grew up in Winnipeg, spending much of his winter youth on the outdoor rinks of the Manitoba city. "They had this playground where they had little shacks that the parks board put up. They had a little shack and a rink with six- or eight-inch boards. There was a caretaker and a stove in the middle of the shack and you could skate there all day long. That's where I spent most of my time. My dad was overseas for the war and mom worked, so there wasn't much reason to go home."

Asked if the rinks were where he developed his hockey skills, James said it was more of a case of learning the right mindset. "I don't think it was skill. I think it was perseverance. You spent hours, and hours, and hours trying to perfect whatever you had."

In James' case, he didn't have a lot. "I remember playing with a stick spliced together with two pieces of board because we couldn't afford a new stick," he said.

Still, James was doing something well enough that the Toronto Maple Leafs scout started watching him closely by the time he was 13 or 14. He recalled one incident with the scout which has stuck with him for some 60 years. "It was around Christmas one time. He [the scout] came up to me and shook my hand and wished me a Merry Christmas. When he took his hand away there was a $10 bill in mine. He said, 'buy something nice for your Mother for Christmas'. I thought that was one of the nicest things anybody had ever done."

Having grown up listening to Foster Hewitt on the radio doing Leaf games, James was already a fan, so when offered an opportunity to sign a "C" form "which made you a Leaf forever and ever Amen!" as he put it, he took the $100 signing bonus and inked the deal. "People asked me why I would do that and tie myself to the Leafs like that. It was because I wanted to play for the Leafs anyway."

So James headed to Toronto at the age of 16, arriving at the train station and finding no one there to meet him. "I wandered around asking people where Maple Leaf Gardens was," he said. Once he found the fabled arena, he walked in and said "here I am," to which the reply was "and who are you?"

So he wasn't exactly a known figure in the Leaf plans, but he would end up playing junior for the Toronto Marlboros, earning all-star recognition his final season, an accomplishment he said, "because I never figured I was all-star material."

James' final year of junior also earned him a one-game call-up when Leaf Eric Nesterenko was injured. "It was against the Montreal Canadiens in the Forum on a Wednesday night. What a thrill that was. I think the Canadiens won the game 1–0. It was just so exciting to live your dream."

As a Marlboro, James was afforded tickets to sit in the press-box and watch Leaf games "... We never had TV back then to watch games. To be able to see it in real life was such an experience."

In the fall of 1956, James joined the Leafs on the ice. He said he was given the opportunity because the team needed a physical presence and he was willing to provide it. "They didn't have anybody else to do that. I didn't have any questions about doing it," he said.

It was a role he had learned in junior with the Marlboros. James recalled one night playing the Hamilton Red Wings where Howie Young, a future NHL tough guy, was playing. That night Young was making his presence felt against several key Toronto players. "Turk Broda our coach came over and told me 'go out and look after Howie will you?'" said James. After he had served his five minutes for fighting, James came back to the bench, and again Broda came over to him. "He told me, 'next time, wait till they drop the puck'."

By the time James was with the Leafs, he was also in the CFL, but he said it was hockey he's proudest of succeeding at. "I didn't have the natural ability in hockey that I did in football. In hockey it was more of a lot of hard work and dedication to doing what it took to be there."

Despite toiling in two leagues, James said the transition from season to season was quite easy.

"No, it wasn't tough on the body. It was the different leg action," said James. Football required an up and down, mortar action, while hockey required a far easier side to side stroke.

And the seasons were shorter. Hockey was only 70 games, plus a maximum of two seven-game playoff rounds. The CFL added another 16 games to the regime, but they were easy ones, said James. "We were coached so much with [Bud] Grant there that our only ambition was to achieve the Grey Cup. Everybody had that goal. It was a walk in the park."

The strain may not have been as great as one would expect, but there were certainly differences between football and hockey players 30 years ago. "Hockey players and football players were different, and I never understood why. Football players seemed to be more rough and ready. Hockey players seemed to be more suit and tie. Maybe it was their upbringing," said James, who was a member of the 1954–55 Memorial Cup champion Toronto Marlboros.

The difference was brought home the first time James walked into Maple Leaf Gardens to play junior hockey. "The first year I went down to Toronto to play junior, I went to Maple Leaf Gardens for a practice, with a windbreaker, a sports shirt, slacks and they said go home and change," said James. James climbed back on the street car, rode across town and put on a suit and tie. "That was the last time I went to the Gardens without a suit and tie on. That was their philosophy," he said.

Getting a start in pro football was also different back in James' playing days. "I came out of high school football and played pro football and you would never do that today. The kids are too smart, they go the college route," he said.

When he joined the Bombers in 1953, the son of former CFL Eddie "Dynamite" James, also a CFL hall of Fame inductee, was the youngest player in the division at 17 years of age.

In 1981 the Hall of Fame called. It was a longer wait than he expected, but he has no regrets as he looks back on the induction. "You just have to wait your turn. It takes time, plus you have to have a good guy to speak for you, and I had a couple of friends in Winnipeg, Jack Matheson and Jack Wells, who were in my corner and kept pushing and pushing," said James, inducted into the Hall of Fame in 1981.

"The night of the dinner, it was quite emotional. It was nice, quite an honour."

Now watching football from the armchair, James said there will still be a CFL decades from now, despite the league's current shakiness. "I think the CFL is merchandising themselves a lot better. They've started to realize they can't fight the beach weather on Friday and Saturday night," said James. People simply aren't willing to disrupt a family weekend at the lake to drive back to the city for a football game, he added. With more mid-week games, the CFL has a better chance of attracting those fans.

"We have a great product here. We have to merchandise it. The best thing that has happened lately is that they're starting to go out and get guys like Doug Flutie and the Rocket," he said. "When I played they had guys like Billy Vessels, who was a Heisman Trophy winner, Johnny Bright, another trophy winner, and Frankie Albert who was an outstanding quarterback, who were all name players."

On the ice, James is also a supporter of the recent action the NHL Players Association took by striking. "They should have done it 35 years ago. It's too bad they didn't, because that's when things were really bad. Guys like Glenn Hall were making $7,000, a $100 a game for 70 games, and that was it," said James.

"I had guys coming up to me who were scoring 20 and 25 goals a year asking me how they could get more money, because I was making more money than they were, and that was because I was playing football," he said.

Football gave James leverage to pry extra money from the Leafs. If he didn't like a contract offer, he could always fall back on football. "Twenty- or 30-goal scorers were pretty hard to find. We were actually a gutless bunch. I wouldn't mind going on strike because I had something to fall back on with football, but these other guys didn't have diddley," he said.

James was lucky. He was actually among the first of the rough and rugged hockey players that are now part of all NHL franchises. "In the old days they only used to go with three lines. When I was there [Toronto] with Imlach in '58, '59 and '60, the fourth line really became important, where they'd throw this line out maybe for two shifts a period to change the momentum around or stir things up a bit."

Also, the stars needed the break, in a time without the automatic television commercial breaks that are now a part of the game, he added. Once in a while, the checking line, including center Duke Edmundson and ironman Johnny Wilson, who played over 500 consecutive games, got a chance to shine.

In the 1960 Stanley Cup final, which Montreal eventually won in four straight games, Toronto coach Punch Imlach was willing to try anything to score a goal in game four, said James. "Imlach was really desperate so he put our line out, and I think we played six, seven, eight minutes of the third period and had three, four or five really great scoring chances, and really got things going," he said.

Following his pro career, James didn't fade from sports. Instead he took up coaching in the Saskatchewan Junior Hockey League. "It really allowed me to keep in contact. I had some really good experiences with a lot of players," James said. "A lot of players who played either hockey or football play till they stop and then there's a big void."

James' coaching career touched some pretty good players. He coached Brian Propp as a 16-year-old and he led the SJHL in scoring, recalled James. A year later Propp was with Brandon of the Western Hockey League when the Yorkton Terriers lost in the SJHL final. "If we'd still have had Propp we'd have won the Centennial Cup," he said.

And there was a special feeling watching Tim Cheveldae from Melville performing in the Detroit Red Wings net. "I was the one who recommended [Tim] Cheveldae to Winnipeg, [then in the WHL]," said James. "I said this kid playing in Melville is a good prospect, so they put him on their players list." When the team transferred to Moose Jaw, they let Cheveldae go, and he was picked up by the Saskatoon Blades.

James also became known as a hard-nosed coach in the Saskatchewan Junior Hockey League, starting with Yorkton where he was team owner as well.

When it came time for fans of the Yorkton Terriers to choose their all stars of the millennium, they turned back the pages on the team's history to the early years of the 1980s.

Six of the seven first-team all stars came from that era. It was a time where the Terriers evolved from perennial losers to league champions. It was a course set by coach Gerry James in the 1980–81 season. James himself admits some surprise in his selection to the club, given the stormy relationship he had with Yorkton fans when he was owner of the junior Terriers. "They loved to hate me, I know that," said James from his current home in Nanoose Bay, B.C. "I don't think the situation I was in at the time was ideal. Private ownership just can't make it in junior jockey. Community-owned teams are much more successful."

That being said, James would build a winner, bringing the Terriers their first league championship before selling his team and moving on. The process of building a winner began in 1980.

James put the credit with the players themselves. "I had some good players," he said in an interview at the time the Millennium team was introduced at a Terrier game early in 2000. "It was a credit to me to be involved as coach with the players I had. We had some great players and we were drawing fans really well, 12, 13, 1,400 a game."

James said while players from the era would go on to set scoring records which stand until today, it was not James' style to stress offence, it was actually the opposite. "I always tried to coach a defensive type team," said James. "But to keep players enthusiastic to play, you have to give them some offensive things to do.

"But I didn't play hockey very well when I played [including with the NHL Toronto Maple Leafs] so I had to concentrate on things like backchecking...things that kept me in the NHL."

James said he understands that as a coach he could do things a player could not, including influencing things before and after games, something he often did by stirring the pot with fans and media. "I came to realize after the things I was doing took the pressure off the players and let the players just go out and play," he said.

The tough stance was one players learned to respect, and to respond to. James said he just tried to bring order to things for his young players. "I think I always tried to be straight with them, and let them know what I was thinking. Young players, even in Junior have to know the parameters within which they are playing, and they're looking for guidance in that."

James said defining expectations for young men in both hockey and in off-ice activities helps them develop on the ice and off. "And there were consequences to pay if you didn't."

Juniors' Best Includes Saskatchewan Pair

Over the years, Canada has put together some outstanding hockey teams for international play. Still, at the junior level there may never have been a team as talented from top to bottom as the Canadian team which won the 2005 World Junior Championship.

Among the talented players on the roster were two players from Saskatchewan, Ryan Getzlaf, who played in the Western Hockey League with the Calgary Hitmen, and Brayden Coburn from the Portland Winter Hawks.

The Canadian team was favoured going in, and didn't disappoint in winning the gold. "It was awesome," said Getzlaf, who was playing in his second straight World Juniors Championships with Team Canada.

For second-year players like Getzlaf, the tournament was almost a mission from the outset. "I think for the guys that came back there was a feeling the first year [2004] we had it and let it slip away." Team Canada lost 4–3 to the United States in the tournament held in Helsinki, Finland.

Coburn said just the chance to try out for the Junior team was a thrill. "It's pretty clichéd to say, but I was one of those guys come Christmas day I'd open the presents, and the rest of the day I was glued to the television watching junior games. I lived and died with every goal." The opportunity to try out for Team Canada was a dream come true for Coburn. "It was my chance to play in the World Junior Championships. I had dreamed about it, but it always seemed so far away."

When organizers called him at 17 in 2003, he was more than a little in awe. "I was pretty surprised I got invited at 17, and only my second year in the WHL. It was really exciting to show them what I could do…But I knew I had a huge hill to climb to make it."

Coburn wouldn't quite climb the hill, being cut the final day of camp, but he took it in stride. In fact, he used it to help him focus the rest of the season back in Portland.

When he was asked to tryout again in the fall of 2004, he was hungry, especially on hearing Brian Sutter was coach. "I got really excited. I knew things were going to start off on the right foot," he said. He felt the 2005 team was going to be good from the outset. "We had a lot of returning guys, a lot of really good players.

"It was actually a really intense camp for anyone who was there."

Coburn was highly motivated from the outset. "It meant a lot to me. Obviously I came up short the year before and I was itching to get a second chance."

The Canadian team was deep in talent, bolstered by the fact that several players were on the roster who might have been playing in the National Hockey League if not for the lock-out that wiped out the 2004–05 pro season. Getzlaf was among those players, having had thoughts of playing with the Anaheim Mighty

Ducks who drafted him 19th overall in 2003. "Every time something happens there's another opportunity," he said.

Getzlaf felt the level of talent in camp, but still felt his experience on the 2004 team gave him a good opportunity to make the club again. "Being my second year, I had a pretty good feeling that I just had to show up and play my game," he said.

"It was the best camp I've been to. The group of guys that was there was unbelievable...It was a pretty high calibre group. There were 10 or 11 guys that might have been playing in the NHL this year had they had the opportunity."

This time Coburn made the team too, and while he felt the team was strong, no one on the roster was thinking about the possibility they were the best junior team this country ever iced. "I don't think anyone was really thinking like that. We just had a job to do. We really wanted to win. That was really our job. We just wanted to be the best team at the tournament."

The level of talent brought with it a level of expectation as well. "I think we went in there with a pretty big load on our shoulders," said Getzlaf, who added that isn't unusual being part of a Canadian team, something he had been involved with for a number of years since playing on the Under-17 team. "That pressure is always there playing for Team Canada. Everybody expects gold."

In spite of pressures and expectations, the team came together smoothly. Getzlaf said it helped that many players had played together through various levels on international play. "There was a good chemistry."

Certainly, the Canadian media were quick to start comparing the 2005 team with the best-ever from this country or any other. "We didn't hear all that stuff too much," said Getzlaf. "We tried to stay away from listening too much to the media."

At the same time, every time Canada played in the tournament, the team's aura grew, although Getzlaf admitted most games were tighter than final scores indicated. "Every game started out tough. We didn't come out of the first period with too big a lead in any of the games," said Getzlaf.

But the system worked because every player was dedicated, and knew what was expected of them. "We had the right mix of guys to do the right jobs," said Getzlaf, "We had four lines all doing it."

The Canadians started hot and stayed that way. "We were so well-prepared, so sure of our jobs and what we had to do," said Coburn. "We just wanted to play our best every game." That, Coburn said, went back to the motivation of coach Sutter. "If you didn't pull your weight, you'd be sitting," he said.

As the wins rolled up, Coburn said the team felt they were playing as they believed they should. "We expected to win. Anything less than that was going to be a failure for us... We were so confident, so well-prepared we felt if we just played our game and did our jobs we'd come out with that win."

The toughest challenge proved to be the semi-finals against Czechoslovakia for a berth in the gold medal game, a game Canada won 3–1. The win was a confidence builder for the team.

The final was less close, as Canada toppled Russia 6–1. The game was close for the opening 20 minutes, Canada leading only 2–1 after the first, but four unanswered goals in the second put the gold around Team Canada's neck.

Coburn said the Canadian game plan in every game was to wear down the opposition. "And I thought that's what we were doing to the Russians. We knew what we had to do."

Playing the Russians was big, given the history of hockey between the two countries, although many on Team Canada were hoping to face Team USA. "A lot of guys were hoping to avenge the loss to the U.S. [in 2004], and beat them on their home ice."

In the end, though, the win was all that mattered. "I was just so excited. There were so many emotions running through you. You just wanted to scream and shout and hug guys.

"A lot of work culminated in achieving what we had wanted to do. We knew what we wanted to do, and we'd finally got it done."

Getzlaf was all smiles about winning gold after settling for silver a year earlier. "It was unbelievable. It was the highlight of my career so far," he said. "I think it was even sweeter because I'd been on both sides of the red line, getting the silver medals in the year before."

It helped the World Championships were being held right across the border in North Dakota, meaning Canadian fans flocked to games. "The whole rink was packed with Canadian people and the energy they had...that made it really special," said Coburn. "It was really fun to play with that atmosphere."

Both players found the championships a highlight, having grown up in love with hockey from an early age.

Getzlaf grew up in Regina, playing many sports, "but hockey was the thing I had the passion for," he said. It was a sport he worked at to be a good player. "I had to work at it when I was a kid."

It was similar for Coburn. "I grew up in Shaunavon. I lived right down the street from the rink, so I was there everyday," said Coburn.

Coburn said his father and grandfather were hockey players, so picking up the stick was partly genetics. "It was kind of the thing to do...I probably started skating around with a chair when I was three years old." That was while the family was still in Frontier. They had moved to Shaunavon by the time Coburn started minor hockey, so he played there until he was a Bantam.

At that point Coburn moved away to hone his hockey career, heading to Notre Dame in Wilcox, which was somewhat interesting given his first experience at the fabled hockey factory and school. "My grandpa sent me to a hockey school there when I was 10 years old. I didn't have the greatest time. I missed home a lot." But Coburn's attitude changed when he was in Grade 9, and the opportunity to move came. "I was pretty excited. I was so pumped about the experience."

The expectation was matched by the reality. "It was just awesome. The two years I was there I enjoyed it so much.

"Everybody there becomes a family. You go to the rink with them. You go to school with them. It's the whole Notre Dame tradition."

Even weeks after the gold medal win in North Dakota, with many hockey people tagging the team the best-ever junior group, Coburn remains modest. "That's hard to say because there's been so many great players on Canadian World Junior teams."

The gold medals are something Coburn said he hopes to build on in his hockey. "It just gives me more confidence as a player. That's an experience I can pass along to my teammates."

Coburn also hopes the gold medal experience helps as he eyes an NHL career, having been drafted by Atlanta eighth overall in 2003. He said the draft was a huge thrill, with his whole family with him in Memphis. "It was the first time we'd had a family vacation in a long time." He added the experience was humbling too. "Looking down and seeing all the NHL people was a bit intimidating. I really didn't know what was going to happen."

Getzlaf too has his sights clearly set on a career in Anaheim, having attended the Mighty Ducks camp in the fall of 2003, and their rookie sessions in 2004. "I felt good at the camps, and I think I've gotten better since my first camp," he said. Being a Duck came as a surprise, having gone later in the draft than expected, and to a team that had never talked to him previous to the selection. However, he said it was never a case of worrying about where he went, but rather working to succeed with whichever team selected him. "And California's not a bad place to live," he added with a laugh.

Looking at the NHL lock-out, Getzlaf said the year may also be a long-term benefit to his career, just as the gold medal win was. "It never hurts anybody to come back and play in Junior again," he said.

Once an Oiler...

When it comes to the idea of "Guts and Go" few players exemplify those attributes on the ice more than the 18-season NHL career of Kelly Buchberger. Growing up in a smaller community like Langenburg was something Buchberger now looks back on as a big benefit in terms of his hockey development, helping set the foundation of grit and determination. "Coming from a small town probably helped me. I grew up only a block away from the rink. I got lots of ice time." By contrast, he said in big cities ice time can be pretty tightly scheduled, whereas in Langenburg "you could go skate just about anytime you wanted."

Time at the rink began early for Buchberger. "I think I was about three years old when I started skating... Then I was always on the ice every day."

Even when he didn't walk the block to the rink, Buchberger said he was likely playing the game. "There was lots of road hockey and shinny, and that all helped improve your skills."

It was the camaraderie and competition of his neighbourhood friends that fueled Buchberger's initial interest in the sport. "Our family didn't have anybody playing really competitive hockey to kind of follow," he said.

By an early age Buchberger's skills were developing at a rate just above the norm for most kids his age. By Pee Wee he was starting "to elevate my play." In the world of hockey, when the cream rises, it's usually shipped off for more refinement, and in Buchberger's case that meant packing his bags at a very early age. At 14, he was on his way to Moose Jaw. "Obviously, I was homesick at the start, but I was skating every day, and you were doing something you love."

The toughest adjustment was switching from a small town school to one in Moose Jaw, but that transition was eased a bit by having teammates going to the same new school.

From Moose Jaw, Buchberger moved back closer to home for a season in the Saskatchewan Junior Hockey League, which in many ways helped him emerge as a potential pro. However, the road to the Melville Millionaires was not exactly smooth. "That year I had tried out for Yorkton [the Terriers] but got released in training camp," he said.

So it was back to Moose Jaw to try out with the Canucks, with no guarantee of a spot on the roster. "Melville called and said I could play there," he said. The decision to join the Millionaires "was a great stepping stone. I learned a lot." His teachers in Melville were Wilf Karius and Sonny Famulak.

A year of seasoning with the Mills, and Buchberger headed back to Moose Jaw to join the then-expansion Warriors in the Western Hockey League.

The team struggled through its first season, a year that included an old problem cropping up and causing Buchberger to miss nearly 30 games, a string that affected where he would be drafted in the spring of 1985.

When Buchberger was seven, his one leg and foot were burned in a fire, leaving his foot tender enough that whenever he wore a skate it would bleed. It was a situation he simply persevered through for a long time before he "learned how to wear my skates so my foot and leg wouldn't bleed." Buchberger never saw the situation as limiting. "It happened at such a young age it was just something I dealt with my whole life to play the same."

But as a first-year Warrior the leg acted up. "My burnt leg got infected around Christmas," he said. It was serious enough to require surgery, and took him out of a big chunk of games. "It affected when I was drafted," he said, although in retrospect things worked out pretty well.

Back in 1985, the National Hockey League draft was not the high-media event it is today. Buchberger said he never attended the draft at all. "Back then you never knew where you'd go. I was back here in Langenburg waiting for a phone call, but I never did get a call," he said. "I heard the team I went to on the radio." He said it was nearly a month before he had mail contact from the Edmonton Oilers, who had selected him in the ninth round, 188th overall.

The start of the Oiler and Buchberger relationship might not have appeared a case of love at first sight, but for the young player from Langenburg, his first Edmonton camp would create a believer out of him. "I went to camp in 1985, the year I was drafted. The energy and atmosphere was so high at training camp," he said. That made him recognize he'd joined an organization dedicated to winning. "I couldn't have been happier to be drafted by a team with such leaders willing to teach young players.

"It was just a pleasure to skate with all those guys in practice and to play an exhibition game."

Buchberger would get only one exhibition game as he attended his first Oiler camp, but he was destined to return to Moose Jaw, where the second-year team under coach Barry Trapp started to make some noise, in large part due to their new bench boss. "Barry, he was a good coach. He was a player's coach. The players loved to play for him. He got the best out of everybody."

With his Junior career complete, Buchberger eyed the pros more closely, and knew he had a hill to climb to break into an Edmonton Oiler roster deep in talent. "Breaking that lineup was no easy task," he said. He'd spend two seasons in the American Hockey League before sticking full-time in "The Show."

Buchberger said the key to making it as an Oiler was fitting into the system the way it was designed. Generally the team drafted players they felt fit the mold. "They wanted players with heart and the desire to do anything for the team. They wanted guys where the team came first.

"If you didn't fit in you were quickly erased from the equation."

With the type of player the Oilers drafted, and then helped define through their system, it's no wonder Buchberger said he has always felt he was an Oiler, even after his pro career took him to several other stops in the NHL. "The Oilers have a saying in the dressing room, 'once an Oiler, always an Oiler'," he said.

That feeling of closeness with the franchise comes from the atmosphere surrounding the team, and the city in which it resides. "It's a smaller city. The players spend a lot of time together. The families spend a lot of time together," said Buchberger. He believes any player who has played in Edmonton found it a special place to play.

It didn't hurt that Buchberger earned two Stanley Cup rings as an Oiler either. He was with the team as they won in both 1988 and in 1990 (he was with the club in '87 but had not played enough games), and admitted it was the highlight of his career. "The first time I carried the Stanley Cup around had to be the best," he offered. Just playing in the NHL has always been a thrill through more than 1,200 career regular season and playoff games.

"When you lace up your skates every night to play in the NHL, it's a thrill."

It didn't hurt having some key role models to follow on the Oilers either. Buchberger said clearly the best player he ever lined up with was Wayne Gretzky. "There's no question the way he was able to read the game, the way he worked at it, the way he played," said Buchberger. "The Great One" was also a class act off the ice as well. Gretzky led by example because he never took a night off.

Another player Buchberger kept a close eye on was Mark Messier, a guy who blossomed into a future Hall of Fame career as an Oiler. "There was no better leader than Mark, the way he played the game. He was unbelievable in practice. He was unbelievable off the ice, and in the way he played the game. He worked harder than probably anybody else on the ice."

For Buchberger, Messier became a player he's tried to emulate as he himself was awarded the Captain's "C." "I tried to follow a lot of guys," said Buchberger, pointing to other Oiler Captains such as Kevin Lowe, Craig MacTavish and Lee Fogolin. In each case there were commonalities Buchberger said he has tried to follow. "The team always came first," he said. As Captains, "they'd do anything for anyone on the team."

Of course not every mentor for Buchberger was a teammate. One was a sibling, his sister Kerri Buchberger, who achieved international status as a volleyball player, including being a member of the Canadian team attending the 1996 Summer Olympics in Atlanta. "We're very close. We've spent a lot of time talking," he said. Watching her play volleyball helped him keep focused on hard work. "She gave it everything she had every night she was out there."

Buchberger admitted if one lived in a perfect world, he would have stayed an Oiler for his entire career, but that was not to be, and after the 1998–99 season, he was left unprotected by

Edmonton. He was quickly chosen in the expansion draft by the fledgling Atlanta Thrashers.

The move to an expansion franchise was a mix of positives and hard times on the ice. While management treated everyone in excellent fashion, losing was an all-too-common occurrence. "Every time we were finding a way to lose," said Buchberger. "Everybody on that team played their hearts out, but we always seemed to come up short."

Before his first season with the Thrashers was over, Buchberger was moved to Los Angeles, then on to Phoenix and Pittsburgh, before becoming a free agent again just before the lock-out of 2004–05.

The moves late in his career never bothered Buchberger, who has taken them as positively as possible. "One thing, you're always wanted somewhere," he said. It was also a case of just being happy playing hockey. "One thing for me is I just love the game. I've enjoyed being a part of the game every night."

The season that never was saw Buchberger gravitate back to Edmonton, where he went behind the bench of the Oilers farm team in the American Hockey League, the Roadrunners. "I didn't want to sit at home during the lock-out," he said. A trial as coach was a good fit, since he sees that as where he will likely end up once his playing days are complete. The experience was a definite learning curve.

"Young players need a lot of support and coaching to get the best out of them," he said. "Obviously, you're dealing with 20 different personalities every night, and trying to get the best out of them."

For a player known for his grit and work ethic, Buchberger has a simple message for young players, pointing to himself as an example of his philosophy. "I always wanted to improve as a player on the ice. One thing, I gave it everything every night."

Buchberger also said for youth, who today have so many options, it's important "to find a passion that they want to pursue, that they love to do." Once you have a passion, then you must work hard to achieve success. "I think that's with anything you do in life. You've got to put your mind to it, and put 110 per cent into it every night or you're not going to be successful."

One day, Buchberger would like to find his way back to the Oilers. "We've been gone for five years, but we never have sold our house...I always wanted to come back for one last year, but things don't always work out the way I wanted," he said.

It's Not All About Hockey

When you think of Midget hockey at its highest calibre in Saskatchewan, you're likely to think of the name Jim McIntyre.

McIntyre is the long-time owner, manager, coach and jack-of-all trades with the Saskatoon Contacts, a team he took over in 1980 from Don Leedahl. "When I took over they were still playing on Saskatchewan double "A" Midget," he said. He decided to buy the team "because I was interested in Midget hockey, and wanted to see the Contacts stay in hockey."

Soon McIntyre would be among a core group of hockey people in the province who would meet to investigate the potential for taking Midget hockey to another level in the province. "The goal at that time was to see if we couldn't all get to the same level as Notre Dame College," he said.

Notre Dame had such strong teams in part because of its ability to attract players from all across North America. By comparison, teams such as the Contacts were limited to drawing talent from local zones, explained McIntyre.

The move to draw players from anywhere within Saskatchewan was not a change easily accomplished. "We had to lobby the SAHA (Saskatchewan Amateur Hockey Association) of the open zone concept so we could be competitive with Notre Dame," said McIntyre. "But we knew we had to do something different."

The change was good for players too, who now have options in trying to break into AAA Midget hockey. "If you believe in yourself you have 12 different places [the number of teams in the league] to go and try to fit in," said McIntyre.

Clearly the move to opening up recruiting for AAA Midget teams to anywhere in the province has been a success as witnessed by how well the league has done on the national scene. "Over the last 20 years everybody pretty well has had a go at going to regionals or on to nationals," he said, pointing to clubs such as the Tisdale Trojans, Beardy's Blackhawks, Notre Dame Hounds and others who have been successful. "It's been an excellent move as far as I'm concerned in terms of Saskatchewan hockey."

At the same time, McIntyre admits "there's still a lot of people who would like to see it go back to the zone system," but he added the level of play shows that such a move would be a backward one for hockey.

The Contacts too have been highly successful through the years, having gone to the national finals tournament for the now-called Telus Cup three times: 1998, 2000 and 2005. The 2005 version of the Contacts became the most successful, winning the Telus Cup, the first national title for the Contacts, but McIntyre said each team is notable for what it accomplished.

That is the case with the '98 team, which finished fourth in the nation. McIntyre has sent several players across the city to play with the University of Saskatchewan Huskies as they advanced in hockey.

The 2000 club was special for another reason. "The team was built from other teams," said McIntyre. "We had 12 losses starting out the season."

The losses sent McIntyre looking for help, and that meant searching through the players cut from other teams. "We picked up four defencemen from other teams that other guys had cut, because we didn't have anyone doing the job."

By Christmas the team of retreads had jelled into a winning unit, with the first indication of how solid they were becoming at the Mac's Tournament in Calgary. They won the famed Midget tournament with a 1–0 win over the USA Bisons. Billy Thompson, who would go on to be drafted by the Florida Panthers of the National Hockey League in 2001, earned the shut-out. The lone Saskatoon goal was netted by Kelsey Wuensch.

The Mac's win was repeated in 2005, as the Contacts made their way to the Telus Cup. Again the opponents would be American, this time Team Illinois. The end result was a mirror-image of five years earlier, with Saskatoon winning 1–0. David Richard scored the winning goal, while Travis Yonkman had the shut-out in net.

McIntyre said whether his teams won the Mac's or not, he views the Christmas-break tournament as important in a team's development. "It's a big stepping stone. For one thing I use it as a measuring stick."

By Christmas most teams are reaching their stride and get to a level of competitiveness that they may have lacked earlier in the season, said McIntyre. "The competition gets stiffer then." A week at the Mac's playing some of the best teams in Canada and abroad gets you ready for the post-Christmas run to the playoffs.

"It's one of the major tournaments in Canada, and one of

the best-run tournaments in Canada," he said. "And it's really supported by people in Calgary. There were 9,000 at the finals this year [2005]. It's a major event in Calgary at that time of year."

While the Mac's win in 2005 showed the Contacts were on the right path, McIntyre said he knew from the outset of the season he had something special to work with as a team. He saw the talent "probably from the last day we got out of training camp." It was a training camp deep in young talent. "We had to let some pretty good hockey players go."

One item of pride for McIntyre is that as good as the Contacts proved to be in 2005, it was with a lot of players who had gone under the radar. There were 14 players on the roster that had not been selected in the Western Hockey League Bantam draft.

It helped that some players who had expected to play up in junior filtered back to the Contacts, something McIntyre said isn't bad for the players either. "It's a time when some kids aren't ready to leave home. They come back here so they can mature a little bit," he said. "It helped them as individuals."

That is an important part of McIntyre's team philosophy. He wants to see his players grow both on and off the ice. "It is a big goal for us. I like to see kids become successful in life, and that's not all about hockey.

"We want to see them contributing to their community, their province and their country." With that in mind, McIntyre added this year when the team headed east to play in the Telus Cup the team was taken to the Parliament Buildings in Ottawa to instill that feeling of being part of the country beyond the game. "You have to express to them how important the community is, and what part in the community they have."

Hockey is a sport that instills ethics which can be carried beyond the rink, said McIntyre. "It teaches you a lot of lifetime skills." Players must have the desire to learn skills such as passing and skating, but it goes farther with the ups and downs of the game mimicking life, and requiring character and toughness players will need away from the game too, he said.

When it came to character, McIntyre said the Contacts showed it in the Telus Cup final when he had two players dressed who had separated shoulders: Scott Brownlee and Pat Cey. "They had a lot of character. I like kids with character. I like kids who will stand up for themselves.

Winning the Telus Cup 4–1 over host Gatineau was obviously the icing on the season, with Nick Kalnicki leading the way for Saskatoon with one goal and two assists, including the game winning goal on a power play. McIntyre said the final went the Contacts' way after a close opening 10 minutes, when the Contacts scored two goals only 22 seconds apart to take a 2–0 lead.

But McIntyre said the toughest competition of their playoff run was in the Saskatchewan AAA Midget Hockey League final against the Notre Dame Hounds. The best-of-five series went to game five and beyond, with Saskatoon winning 2–1 in double overtime of game five on a goal by Kyle Bortis. "Notre Dame had a pretty good team," said McIntyre, who added goaltender Yonkman was the difference, just as he had been at the Mac's. "He had a knack of coming prepared to play final games," he said.

With the success McIntyre and the Contacts have had, it means a lot of talented players have passed through the program. "Over the years I've had the opportunity to be involved with a lot of good athletes," he said, pointing out seven or eight who have gone on to play in the NHL. "I've had a lot of good kids, but the most successful to this point would be Jeff Friesen, who was drafted 11th overall by the San Jose Sharks in 1994, and has since played a decade in the league. I knew he was a good hockey player."

On the 2005 roster there are a couple of players who may

match Friesen's success. "I've got a couple on this team that would match him. Kyle Bortis, I don't think you could find a better player. Eric Gryba is up there too," said McIntyre.

To help develop young players and find team success, McIntyre has had to have good people around him. "You've got to have people who share your philosophy," he said. Something must be working, as he has ex-parents scouting for him for 15 to 20 years after their kids played on the team.

McIntyre also draws on a lot of veteran advice as a coach, and that includes playing at the Schroh Arena. "I play in a museum," said McIntyre, pointing to players such as Jackie McLeod, a member of the International Hockey Hall of Fame, and Bobby Dawes, who played in the same barn in the oldtimers' league.

Over the years the Contacts have had success on the ice, but McIntyre said owning an AAA Midget team is far from a financial windfall. "You should see how my wife looks when she gets the VISA bill," he joked. "...It's not easy to raise money for a team like this. It's the same old story. We don't really help athletes in this country, even at the Olympic level. If an athlete gets there [to the Olympics] it's their own efforts and fundraising. There's a great bureaucracy in our country and they're not spending it on the athletes."

McIntyre's Contacts, and the cross-city Saskatoon Blazers are the only privately held teams in the Saskatchewan AAA Midget Hockey League, and he can understand why. At the same time, he said the two Saskatoon teams have accomplished much. "It certainly has been a major factor in Saskatoon. Having two teams of this calibre, it makes the minor hockey system better," he said.

That's why the 2005 Telus Cup was so sweet. "It makes me happy it came back to Saskatoon. There have been two teams trying for an awfully long time to accomplish that."

Earning Your Stripes

If you lace up a pair of skates as a kid growing up in Saskatchewan, you probably dream of playing in the National Hockey League. Not every young dreamer makes it to the big show as a player, but for some there is another avenue to skating in the NHL.

Brad Meier and Mark Wheler grew up in Saskatoon and Battlefords respectively. Both learned to skate at a young age, playing minor hockey through the local ranks. Today, both skate regularly in the NHL, although neither's playing skills were good enough to achieve such success. Meier is now an NHL referee, while Wheler patrols the ice as a linesman.

The two officials have a long-time connection, going back to sharing a place through the university years, while both were also honing their skills on the ice, to working together in the NHL.

Both also share a somewhat similar start in the game of hockey, following in the footsteps of family. "I was actually born in the [United] States," explained Meier. "My dad [Ron] played in the old International Hockey League."

Meier senior would toil in the IHL for four seasons, most of that time with the Dayton Gems, and then move the family back to Saskatoon where Brad would learn the game. Brad would become a defenceman like his father, but he admitted the skill level was just never there, even with the advice of his dad on the position. He said he played right up to Junior, but then came to a realization. "I played one game of Junior "B" and realized I wasn't going anywhere as a player," he said.

So, Meier turned his attention to another skill he had been learning since he was 12, that of an official. He said he'd donned the striped sweater to earn a few dollars, and as he saw any playing dreams fade, the stripes were a way to "help pay my way through school."

Turning away from the game to officiate was not something that bothered Meier's father, even though he'd been a player. "He never pushed me as a kid to play. I think he respected the fact I could pursue it to the level I did," said Brad.

For Wheler, hockey was something that came easy as something to do while very young, living only a couple of blocks from the old Battlefords Arena. "For the first couple of years it was natural ice in the old arena—it's a furniture store now."

While playing the game was an obvious choice, so too was picking up the whistle as a linesman at the age of 13. "My older brother Ken was a referee in the Western Canada Hockey League, and worked in the Sask Junior before that," said Mark. "He ended up under contract to the NHL at one point, so I looked at officiating as something worth pursuing."

By 16, Mark was officiating in the Sask Junior league himself. He said he believes he made the jump as young as he did because of his older brother. "I was helped by my brother having been there. They knew who I was."

In 1983, Wheler moved to Saskatoon and took at job at Sears

changing tires and batteries, a job he got from Don Cornwell, who appreciated he was a hockey official too. "He let me work there and work in the Western [Hockey] League."

While the arrangement was working well, Wheler decided it was time to go to university. "Again that was advice from my brother," said Wheler. Older sibling Ken explained that while there might be a future as an official, it doesn't always work out, as he learned having only refed in a few exhibition contests, and linesing a handful of regular season games. "He [Ken] said 'don't put all your eggs in one basket'," said Brad.

So Wheler attained his Bachelor of Commerce with a major in marketing, while continuing to officiate, and bunking with Meier and a third hockey official Brent Rieber. The three would become great friends. In fact Meier and Wheler were best men at each other's weddings.

Wheler said he believes the time the trio lived together was what laid the foundation for their future officiating success—Rieber has officiated in Japan and Europe.

"When I think back when Brad, Brent and I lived together we all had a little different set of skills. We learned from each other," said Wheler. "... We talked for a long time some evenings after games. I think that's when we sort of asserted ourselves as guys that can do this game."

Meier said while he found he enjoyed officiating, he came to the role by complete accident. "It was kind of a fluke actually," he said, explaining he went to his younger brother's game at the outdoor rink straight from one of his own.

"There was no referee there. They found out I had my skates and told me to go drop the puck," he said. "I had no idea what I was doing. But I made four bucks as a 12-year-old, so I thought 'this is doable'."

"I can honestly say I enjoyed it. At times it got frustrating, but that was mainly at other people's actions," said Meier. It helped that he seemed to progress as an official with each jump in level. "I was fortunate enough to have pretty good success. There was such good mentoring in Saskatoon. Guys who have come through the program in Saskatoon have had pretty good success."

Only once, when the rigours of university and balancing officiating hockey got to be almost too much, did Meier ever contemplate giving up on wearing the stripes.

Certainly there are pressures on officials, especially when they're young, which Meier said you have to learn to block out. "I go and watch a minor hockey game now and hear some of the comments you hear in the stands, not just at officials, but players, and other parents, and I wonder what drives them to act like that in public," he said.

Even in the NHL, Meier has come to the realization he can't satisfy fans. "As an official you end up with half the people hating you, and half the people loving you all night long," he said. It comes down to feeling secure in your abilities. "... You have to go with what got you there."

In the pros, players still yell, but Meier said an elder statesman of the stripes once explained it as "they aren't yelling at you, they're yelling at the jersey."

Wheler said you need to use the prospect of being questioned on a call to make sure you don't make mistakes. "The biggest thing is not to give them room to argue," he said. There is pressure these days "from 18 different camera angles on every play. You have to react to the play and get the best read you can. What can really make or break you is the focus to work your butt off every night right from the start to the finish."

Once through university, Meier joined the Saskatoon fire department, and found the time off afforded a firefighter meshed well with officiating, and he kept developing his skills first in the

Western Hockey League, and then in the now-defunct IHL. "It seemed every time a new opportunity presented itself, I had the time and opportunity to chase it," he said.

Wheler joined the staff of Molson Brewery, and while busy with the career, found time to keep officiating too. "I don't think I could have done the job as easily had I been a referee," he said. "As a linesman you work more home games than as a referee. I remember one season I did the Saskatoon Blades' final 10 games in a row."

The first real taste of success, which hinted at better things to come, was working the Memorial Cup in Saskatoon in 1989.

By 1992, though, Wheler was tiring of the pace of a career with Molson's and trying to officiate as many games as possible. "I'd come home, throw my briefcase down and head off to Prince Albert or wherever to officiate," he said. So Wheler set a goal and a deadline. "I said I'd do all I can this year to make it to the Memorial Cup [in Seattle]," he said. He was thinking he'd hang them up after the season. "I earned a spot at the Memorial Cup, and worked the final game."

Then fate intervened with Ottawa and Tampa Bay joining the NHL. Wheler was hired as one of the new linesmen needed with the expanded team roster. "It was sort of a case of being at the right place at the right time," he said. "But I worked hard to keep that door open. It wasn't a total fluke, but the stars were aligned a little bit for me."

So Wheler made the jump right from the WHL to the NHL, where he admits he was again aided by his older brother's advice. "That made it a little easier," but also added the game was certainly faster. "If you had to stop and think where you have to be, you'll be too late getting there."

While Meier said he enjoyed success, it wasn't until he started working in the Saskatchewan Junior Hockey League that he began to envision officiating as a professional career. "Then, I thought maybe, if the cards fell into place, it might be something I could attain," he said.

So how does an official jump to the NHL? Well, there is no draft as there is for players. Nor do you really apply for the job. Instead, Meier said the league tends to come find you. "They keep tabs on guys they think might be a prospect," he said. "They do more of the hunting than we do. They know who has potential."

As an official you have to do the things to be noticed. "There sort of a network out there. They rely on the opinion of a lot of people," Wheler said. "You have to prove yourself in the league you're working in. You have to show that you can excel at that level, so they'll take notice."

In Meier's case, he was working in the WHL when NHL official representative Brian Lewis approached him. "He said he was happy with the job I did, 'keep working on it, and there might be an opportunity down the road'," he said. "That kind of piques your interest a little bit, and makes you work harder."

For Meier, the break into the NHL came in October 1999, in Pittsburgh. While the initial feeling was "Wow! I finally got here," Meier pointed to an off-ice moment as one of the keenest memories of that game. "Mario [Lemieux] wasn't playing. He was in the press box, and was nice enough to sign my program."

In Wheler's case the thrill of the NHL culminated in the spring of 2004, as he worked Game 7 of the Stanley Cup final. "It was the game I'd been wanting to work since I was 13... You just know it all comes down to that one game.

"Now the trick is trying to get back there [the finals]."

Wheler said that's something fans should recognize about officials. Like players, they are doing their best to get to the playoffs, where only the league's best get to blow the whistle. That motivation means calling the games as best they can, without favouritism. "One thing nobody understands is officials are the only ones in the building who don't care who wins. We're just trying hard every night to make the playoffs too."

Wheler thinks it's great he and Meier get to work together quite often in the NHL, adding at times it brings back memories from years earlier. "You think back to the old stadium working some Junior "B" game on a Sunday afternoon and wondering then where all this is taking you."

More hockey books from Heritage House Publishing

Guts and Go: Great Saskatchewan Hockey Stories
Calvin Daniels

"A great read.... This book scores with profiles of many of the most famous Saskatchewan-born NHL players, and gets a big assist with stories of lesser-known players and teams." Jason Hammond, CJRT Radio
$16.95 paperback. ISBN 1-894384-80-6

The Game of Our Lives
Peter Gzowski

This best-selling hockey classic tells the incredible story of the Edmonton Oilers' 1980–81 season when the team was poised on the edge of greatness.
"This is a classic of hockey writing." The Globe and Mail
$19.95 paperback. ISBN 1-894384-59-8

Going Top Shelf: An Anthology of Canadian Hockey Poetry
Michael P.J. Kennedy, editor

From Michael Ondaatje to Stompin' Tom Connors, readers will delight in this entertaining collection of wonderful hockey poems and song lyrics.
$15.95 paperback. ISBN 1-894384-99-7

Simply the Best: Insights and Strategies from Great Hockey Coaches
Mike Johnston and Ryan Walter

Simply the Best delivers rare insights on success straight from the hearts and minds of winning coaches including Scotty Bowman, Marc Crawford, Jacques Demers, Ken Hitchcock, Pat Quinn, and Mike Keenan. Recognized as the greatest coaches in the game, these "elite 12" openly discuss in their own words strategies that have made them successful.
$24.95 paperback. ISBN 1-894384-81-4

The Battle of Alberta: A Century of Hockey's Greatest Rivalry
Steven Sandor

Even before Alberta was a province, the rivalry between Calgary and Edmonton was in full swing. From the first games in the 1890s up to the thrillers of the 1980s, the rough and tumble relationship between these two hockey hotbeds is presented in all its glory. Illustrated.
$19.95 paperback. ISBN 1-894974-01-8

Ask for these great books at your local bookstore, or visit
www.heritagehouse.ca